Disney

Tim Burton's THE NIGHTMARE BEFORE CHRISTMAS

The Official Cookbook & Entertaining Guide

Disney

Tim Burton's THE NIGHTMARE BEFORE CHRISTMAS

The Official Cookbook & Entertaining Guide

Recipes by Kim Laidlaw
Crafts by Caroline Hall
Text by Jody Revenson

INSIGHT EDITIONS

San Rafael · Los Angeles · London

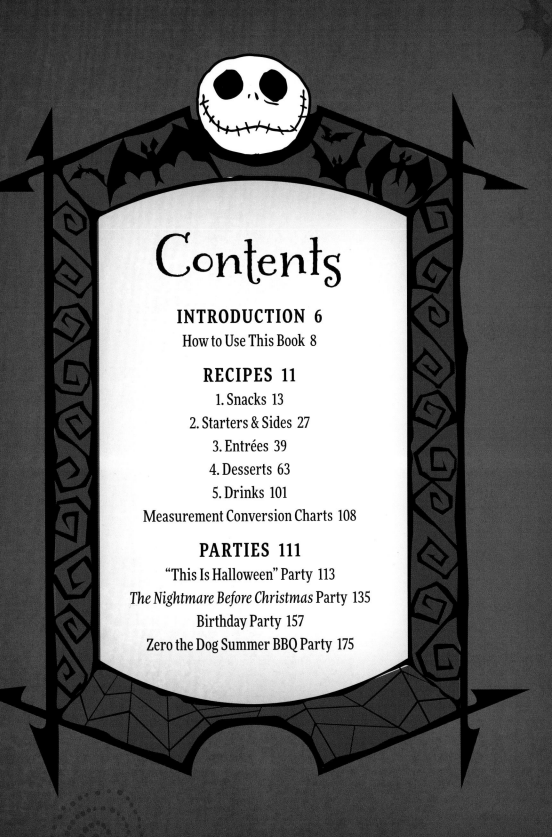

Contents

Introduction

"'Twas a long time ago, longer now than it seems, in a place that perhaps you've seen in your dreams...."

In Tim Burton's *The Nightmare Before Christmas*, Jack Skellington, the Pumpkin King, travels from his world of Halloween Town to Christmas Town. The beautiful Christmas decorations inspire Jack to create a striking combination of two contrasting holidays and leave an indelible mark on millions of people's imaginations.

But, as Jack learns, celebrations and holidays don't just appear out of thin air. Every party takes time and work to make it unique and memorable. When putting together a party—especially a party based on *The Nightmare Before Christmas*—the devil is definitely in the details. But with this entertaining guide, we've made the details easy and enjoyable to achieve, for celebrations of which both Jack Skellington and Santa Claus would be proud.

Setting the scene is key, and the suggestions within this volume will definitely create an electrifying atmosphere reminiscent of Halloween Town or Christmas Town, beginning with the invitations for each party. There are ideas in each chapter for decor, crafts, and favors that have been designed to fulfill each specific occasion, but feel free to make your party your way.

Keep a countdown clock in mind. The inhabitants of Halloween Town keep one that helps them plan ahead (though you probably don't need to start 364 days before the event). Jack may set himself on fire when the holiday ends, but you should not feel as if you're running on fumes when the party starts.

Once you've set your party date, break down what you'll need to do so you can have everything ready before your guests arrive. Invitations, menus, and games are all taken care of here, but make sure you're on top of a schedule to get everything done. Send out invitations in time and consider how to arrange your party space(s) so there's room for everyone to participate in the activities you've planned. Set your menu, buy the ingredients, and figure out what can be made ahead of time. For decorations, see what you already have at home, such as glue and tape and Christmas lights, and make sure you have enough on hand. Then pick up whatever else you'll need to light up electric chairs and create potion bottles.

When Jack decides to make Christmas his, he makes it the Halloween Town way, with gifts that bring screams, less from glee and more from shock. But this approach need not be limited to the five parties suggested here. Be inspired to use any and all of the ideas within to make an everyday dinner not so everyday or to create a movie night that's dreadfully peculiar.

To paraphrase the opening narration of *The Nightmare Before Christmas*, if you've ever wondered where parties come from, we'd say it's time you begun! Enjoy—and have fun!

How to Use This Book

The first section in this book is filled with over fifty recipes for you to mix and match to create your own festive *Nightmare Before Christmas*-themed meal any time of the year.

The second half of this book features five different parties that allow you to celebrate *The Nightmare Before Christmas* all year long.

Each party begins with a handmade invitation for you to create and send to all your guests. After that, it's time to get started planning your decorations! The decor section provides you with a variety of DIY decoration ideas that you can use to spruce up your space. The crafts and favors section includes projects for you to create or set up for your guests to build themselves.

No party is complete without a few extra fun elements! The games section features activities for your guests to participate in and bring *The Nightmare Before Christmas* into your home.

Last but not least, we'll suggest a few recipes from the recipe section that go with each party theme, but you should feel free to mix and match from any part of the cookbook section based on your personal tastes.

There are step-by-step instructions for each recipe, project, and activity to help you successfully complete every element.

Online Resources

Throughout the parties, some of the decor, crafts, and favors in this book are available as downloadable templates that you can print at home. All templates are free and available for download at www.insighteditions.com/NightmareEntertaining. Please refer to this URL whenever you see this symbol ⬇ in the book.

Recipes

Food really sets the flavor of any party, and a party with a specific theme—like Christmas, a birthday, or a summer barbecue—lends itself to an iconic menu. A party with the theme of *The Nightmare Before Christmas* offers frighteningly wonderful possibilities to serve mash-ups of traditional holiday dishes and opportunities for new concoctions based on the characters, locations, and even the songs from the movie.

Every party has a suggested menu, but what you serve is totally up to you. What's this? Jack Skellington Cheese and Veggie Quesadillas accompanied by Homemade Christmas Eggnog? How jolly! Dr. Finkelstein's Bite-Sized "Brain" Puff Pies and Behemoth BBQ Pork Buns on the same plate? Perfectly marvelous. Nothing but desserts? A witch's fondest dream! Similar to the way Jack made Christmas the Halloween Town way, make your menu your own.

No need to sound the howling Black Cat alarm, but a few caveats are included to help you pull off your party like a pro. Before finalizing the food, check to see if any of your guests have dietary restrictions. Make sure there's enough ice for cold drinks, and have coasters or trivets on hand to protect your furniture from damage.

The recipes that follow evoke all the spine-tingling terror of Jack's foray into Christmas without any of the disaster he brought about. There'll be joy and cheer in every bite.

Snacks

Sally Sweet-n-Salty Popcorn

The Mayor Chocolate Pretzel Spiderwebs

Igor Cheesy Breadstick Bones

Dr. Finkelstein Bite-Sized "Brain" Puff Pies

Jack Skellington Black Bean Dip

The Mayor Spider Deviled Eggs

Oogie Boogie Guacamole With Ghost & Christmas Tree Chips

Full Moon Queso Dip

Creature Under the Stairs Tempura Green Bean "Fingers"

Snacks are wonderful finger foods, especially if you have long, bony fingers like Jack Skellington. When your guests need some refreshment after the exhilaration of a challenging game, nibbles and munchies are the best kind of pick-me-ups. Done the Halloween Town way, pretzels become spiderwebs, popcorn is tinted with the colors of Sally's patchwork dress, and breadsticks are shaped like the bone Jack tosses to his dog, Zero. The majority of these recipes don't take long to put together and can be made a day or two before the party. Just make sure you prepare enough, in case your inner Creature Under the Stairs decides to have a midnight nosh

Have fun with plates and bowls—basic black is always a hit, but you can also theme the serving dishes with cutout cat ears or bat wings. Tape bugs or eyeballs around the outside, or place miniature witches' brooms on the side. And don't forget: napkins, napkins, napkins.

Sally Sweet-n-Salty Popcorn

This candy-coated popcorn is just a little bit salty and a lot of fun. The colors are reminiscent of Sally's patchwork dress, and dark licorice pieces are like snips of threading. You'll need a candy thermometer to make sure the sugar is the right temperature. Always be extra careful when working with boiling sugar.

Yield: 4 to 6 servings | Difficulty: Medium

- 3 tablespoons avocado or canola oil
- ½ cup popcorn kernels
- 3 tablespoons unsalted butter
- 1 cup sugar
- ¼ cup water
- 1 tablespoon light corn syrup

- A few drops dark pink or red gel food coloring
- ¼ teaspoon salt, plus more if needed
- A few drops golden yellow gel food coloring
- A few drops teal or blue gel food coloring
- About 6 black licorice twists, cut into 1-inch pieces (½ cup)

1. Preheat the oven to 300°F. Line a large rimmed baking sheet with parchment paper, and set aside.

2. In a large heavy pot over medium heat, add the oil and two kernels of popcorn. Cover and cook until you hear the kernels pop. Remove from the heat, and add the remaining kernels; swirl the pan for about 30 seconds. Cover and continue to cook over medium heat, shaking the pan continuously, until the popping slows to 3 to 5 seconds between pops—this will take a few minutes, so pay close attention to the sound. Remove the pan from the heat, and carefully lift off the lid. Divide the popcorn evenly among three medium heatproof bowls, discarding any unpopped kernels.

3. In a saucepan over medium heat, melt the butter. Add the sugar, water, corn syrup, and salt, then stir gently with a whisk. Bring to a boil, then reduce the heat to low, and simmer until the mixture reaches 238°F (also known as "soft ball stage") on a candy thermometer. Immediately take the pot off the heat, then carefully pour the sugar mixture into 3 small microwave-safe bowls, dividing evenly (about ⅓ cup per bowl).

4. Working quickly, add a different food color to each bowl (one pink, one yellow, and one teal). Stir to combine. If the sugar mixture becomes too thick, heat it in the microwave on high for 10 seconds. One at a time, drizzle one of the colored sugar mixtures over one bowl of popcorn while quickly stirring with a silicone spatula to coat the popcorn as evenly as possible.

5. Spread the coated popcorn on one-third of the prepared baking sheet. Repeat with the other two bowls of popcorn, keeping the popcorn colors separate on the baking sheet.

6. Bake for 15 minutes, stirring once or twice, but don't mix the colors together while stirring. Set the tray aside on a wire rack. Season with a little more salt while warm if you like. Let cool completely. Add the colored popcorn to a large serving bowl. Toss together with the black licorice pieces. Serve.

The Mayor Chocolate Pretzel Spiderwebs

Create these delicious white chocolate webs for spiders to hang out on at your party. This fun project is so easy, but it helps to have a small piping bag for the icing to pipe the web (you can also use a zippered plastic bag with the corner snipped off).

Yield: 8 spiderwebs | Difficulty: Easy

- 64 thin pretzel sticks
- 1¼ cups white chocolate chips
- About 3 tablespoons semisweet chocolate chips

1. Line two large rimmed baking sheets with parchment paper. Lay eight pretzel sticks in a radial circle, like the spokes of a wheel on the paper. Repeat with the remaining sticks. You should be able to fit four to a baking sheet.

2. Place the white chocolate chips in a microwavable bowl, and microwave on high, stirring after every 10 seconds, until melted and smooth. Transfer the melted white chocolate to a pastry bag fitted with a small round tip (about ⅛ inch). Alternatively, transfer the chocolate to a zippered plastic bag and snip a small hole in the bottom corner to create a piping bag.

3. For each spiderweb, pipe a round circle of white chocolate in the center of the spoke (this helps hold the pretzel sticks together), then slowly draw a medium-thick spiral of chocolate out from the center to the ends of the sticks.

4. To make the spiders, place one semisweet chocolate chip, bottom side up, in the center of the white chocolate round on each web (these are the spider bodies). Put the remaining semisweet chocolate chips in a microwavable bowl, and microwave on high in 20-second bursts, stirring after every 20 seconds, until melted and smooth. Transfer the melted semisweet chocolate to a pastry bag fitted with a very small round tip (about ⅟₁₆ inch). Alternatively, transfer the chocolate to a zippered plastic bag, and snip a tiny hole in the bottom corner. For each spider, pipe eight thin legs radiating from the center circle.

5. Refrigerate until set, about 15 minutes. Gently peel away from the parchment paper. Serve at once; these are best served the day they are made.

Igor Cheesy Breadstick Bones

Both Dr. Finkelstein's assistant Igor and Zero would be thrilled to come across these delicious breadstick bones! These are great served on their own, alongside a big bowl of soup or a hearty salad, or with a dish of warm marinara or pesto for dipping.

Yield: 12 bones | Difficulty: Easy

- 1 pound store-bought pizza dough
- 2 tablespoons extra-virgin olive oil
- ⅓ cup grated Parmesan cheese

1. Line a large rimmed baking sheet with parchment paper. Divide the dough into twelve equal pieces (a kitchen scale helps with this). Roll each piece of dough into a rope about 6 to 8 inches long, leaving the ends rounded. Cut the rounded ends of each dough rope in half (about a 1-inch slit) and form into knobs for bones. Space the dough bones evenly on the baking sheet. Gently brush each dough bone lightly with olive oil, then sprinkle with the Parmesan, dividing it evenly.

2. Cover the bones loosely with plastic wrap, and place in a warm, draft-free part of the kitchen. Let rise until puffy, about 30 minutes.

3. While the bones are rising, preheat the oven to 425°F. Bake until golden brown, about 18 minutes. Let cool slightly before serving.

Dr. Finkelstein Bite-Sized "Brain" Puff Pies

These bite-sized pies are made with store-bought puff pastry and filled with a savory sausage stuffing that resembles the Mad Scientist's hinged skullcap and brains. But you don't have to be a mad scientist to make these!

Yield: 22 to 24 mini pies | Difficulty: Medium

- ½ tablespoon avocado oil
- ½ small yellow onion, finely chopped
- ½ pound bulk sweet Italian sausage
- 1 teaspoon minced fresh sage
- 1 teaspoon minced fresh parsley

- 2 large eggs
- ⅓ cup fresh bread crumbs
- Salt and freshly ground black pepper
- Cooking spray
- Two 8-ounce sheets frozen puff pastry, thawed (from one 17-ounce package)

1. Preheat the oven to 400°F. In a frying pan over medium heat, warm the avocado oil. Add the onion and cook, stirring, until it starts to brown, about 5 minutes. Crumble the sausage into the pan and cook, stirring, until browned, about 3 minutes. Drain off the fat, then transfer the mixture to a medium bowl. Stir in the sage and parsley. Let cool slightly.

2. In a small bowl, whisk one egg until well mixed. Add to the sausage mixture along with the bread crumbs. Season with salt and pepper if needed. Mix until evenly combined. Cover and refrigerate until ready to use, up to 2 days in advance.

3. Spray a 24-cup mini muffin pan lightly with cooking spray. On a lightly floured surface, roll out one sheet of the puff pastry until it is ¹⁄₁₆-inch thick. Using a 3-inch-round biscuit cutter or a glass, cut out as many rounds as you can. Press a dough round into each muffin cup. Roll out the second sheet of pastry to ¹⁄₁₆-inch thick. Using a 2-inch-round biscuit cutter or a glass, cut out as many "lids" as you have bases. Continue to cut out 3-inch bases and 2-inch lids until you use up all the dough. You should be able to cut out 22 to 24 of each. Place the lids on a separate plate. Refrigerate for 15 minutes.

4. Divide the sausage mixture evenly among the muffin cups. In a small bowl, beat the remaining egg with 1 teaspoon water. Remove the pastry lids from the refrigerator, and lightly brush one side of the lids. Place a pastry lid, egg side down, on top of each pie. Refrigerate until ready to bake, up to 1 day in advance.

5. When ready to bake, preheat the oven to 400°F. Lightly brush the top of each pie with the remaining egg wash. Bake until puffed and golden brown, about 25 minutes. Let cool slightly in the pan on a wire rack. Pop out each puff pie with a butter knife, and serve warm.

TIP
The pies can be assembled in advance and baked just before serving.

Jack Skellington Black Bean Dip

A warm, bubbling skillet of savory black bean dip topped with plenty of melted cheese will be gobbled up by guests before you can say "Jack Skellington!" This would be great served with the Full Moon Queso Dip (page 24).

Yield: 6 servings | Difficulty: Easy

- 3 tablespoons extra-virgin olive oil
- 1 small yellow onion, finely chopped
- 2 cloves garlic, minced
- 1 teaspoon chili powder
- ½ teaspoon ground cumin
- Two 15.5-ounce cans black beans, drained and rinsed
- ¼ cup chopped fresh cilantro

- 2 tablespoons fresh lime juice
- ½ teaspoon salt
- ¼ cup water
- 4 ounces shredded Monterey Jack cheese (about 1 cup)
- ½ cup whole pitted black olives
- ½ cup halved or quartered cherry tomatoes
- Tortilla chips, for serving

1. Preheat the oven to 425°F. In a small (8-inch) cast-iron or ovenproof pan over medium-low heat, warm 1 tablespoon olive oil. Add the onion and cook, stirring, until golden, about 5 minutes. Stir in the garlic, chili powder, and cumin, and cook until fragrant, about 30 seconds.

2. Transfer the onion mixture to the bowl of a food processor. Set aside 1 cup of the beans, then add the rest of the beans to the bowl of the food processor. Add the cilantro, lime juice, salt, the remaining 2 tablespoons olive oil, and water. Process until smooth.

3. Wipe out the pan, then transfer the bean mixture to the pan. Stir in the remaining beans. Top with the shredded cheese. Bake until the cheese is melted and the bean dip is bubbling, about 15 minutes.

4. Slice half of the olives crosswise and arrange those on top of the cheese to look like Jack Skellington's two large oval eyes. Slice the remaining olives lengthwise and use those to create a wide grinning mouth. Arrange the cherry tomatoes around the edge of the pan. Serve warm with the tortilla chips on the side for dipping.

The Mayor Spider Deviled Eggs

A classic party appetizer, deviled eggs never seem to go out of style. These protein-packed snacks are topped with black olive "spiders" as a nod to the Mayor's arachnid bow tie.

Yield: 24 deviled eggs | Difficulty: Easy

- 1 dozen large eggs
- ⅓ cup mayonnaise
- 1 tablespoon Dijon mustard
- Salt and freshly ground black pepper
- 24 pitted black olives

1. Place the eggs in a large saucepan, and fill the pan with enough cold water to cover the eggs. Bring to a gentle boil over medium heat, then reduce the heat to low, and simmer for 15 minutes. Meanwhile, fill a large bowl with ice and cold water.

2. When the eggs are ready, using a slotted spoon, transfer to the ice bath. Set aside for 10 minutes, until the eggs are cool to the touch.

3. Remove the eggs from the water. Gently tap each egg against a work surface, rolling it back and forth with light pressure, cracking the shell all over. Peel off the shell. Cut each egg in half lengthwise. Scoop out the yolks, and transfer them to a medium bowl. Arrange the egg-white halves on a serving platter.

4. Add the mayonnaise and mustard to the yolks. Use a fork to mash the yolks to a paste. Season with salt and pepper. Spoon the yolk mixture into the egg-white halves, dividing it evenly and forming it into a mound (alternatively, transfer the mixture to a pastry bag fitted with a medium plain round tip, and pipe the yolk mixture into each egg-white half).

5. For each deviled egg, cut an olive in half lengthwise and place one half, cut side down, in the center of the yolk; this is the spider body. Cut the remaining half lengthwise into eight thin slivers to create eight legs, and arrange them on the yolk for the spider legs. Serve at once, or cover and refrigerate for up to 1 day.

TIP
If you like, add a teaspoon of minced fresh parsley or cilantro to the yolk mixture, or sprinkle the spiders with sweet or smoked paprika before serving.

Oogie Boogie Guacamole With Ghost & Christmas Tree Chips

This guacamole is studded with tomato and cilantro "bugs" and couldn't be more Oogie-like. It's easy to make your own tortilla chips by cutting out shapes with cookie cutters and baking until they are crisp. We chose ghosts and Christmas trees, but other shapes, like bugs, would be just as fun to experiment with.

Yield: 6 servings (about 2 cups guacamole) | Difficulty: Easy

FOR THE TORTILLA CHIPS

- Twelve 6-inch corn tortillas
- 2 tablespoons avocado or canola oil
- Salt

FOR THE GUACAMOLE

- 3 ripe avocados, halved and pitted
- ½ cup quartered cherry tomatoes
- 3 tablespoons chopped fresh cilantro
- Juice of 1 large lime
- 1 teaspoon hot pepper sauce
- Salt and freshly ground black pepper

TO MAKE THE TORTILLA CHIPS

1. Preheat the oven to 375°F. Line a large baking sheet with parchment paper. Using a cookie cutter of your choice, cut out as many shapes as you can from the tortillas.

2. Brush the shapes lightly on both sides with the oil, then arrange them in a single layer on the prepared baking sheet. Season with salt. Bake until crisp and golden brown, 10 to 12 minutes. Let the chips cool while you make the guacamole.

TO MAKE THE GUACAMOLE

3. Scoop the flesh from the avocados into a bowl. Using a potato masher or a large fork, smash the avocados until mostly smooth. Stir in the tomatoes, cilantro, lime juice, and hot sauce. Season with salt and pepper, and serve right away with the chips alongside for dipping.

TO STORE

4. Cover the bowl tightly with plastic wrap so that the plastic is touching the guacamole, and refrigerate for up to 1 day.

Full Moon Queso Dip

TIP

Purchase a block of cheese and shred it yourself, since pre-shredded cheese contains additives that keep it from melting into a smooth mixture.

Tex-Mex queso dip is always a great choice for a party, and when it's served in a round fondue pot, the queso looks like a full moon and stays melted without firming up.

Yield: 6 to 8 servings (about 4 cups queso) | Difficulty: Easy

- 1 tablespoon avocado or canola oil
- ½ small yellow onion, finely chopped
- 1 small jalapeño, seeded and minced (optional)
- 1 clove garlic, minced
- One 4-ounce can roasted green chiles, drained
- 1 cup whole milk

- 12 ounces American cheese, shredded or chopped
- 4 ounces Monterey Jack cheese, shredded
- Salt and freshly ground black pepper
- 1 medium tomato, seeded and finely diced
- ¼ cup fresh cilantro, chopped
- Tortilla chips, for serving

1. In a medium saucepan over medium-low heat, warm the oil. Add the onion and cook, stirring, until it starts to brown, about 5 minutes. Add the jalapeño, if using, and garlic, and cook until fragrant, about 1 minute more. Add the green chiles, and stir to combine. Add the milk. When the milk is warm, add the cheeses, stirring until smooth and melted. Season with salt and pepper to taste. Stir in the tomato and cilantro. Continue to simmer until the mixture is hot.

2. To serve, transfer the queso to a wide round bowl for serving. Place on a platter and surround with tortilla chips. Serve at once. If the queso cools too much, it will firm up, so just microwave it in 20-second bursts to reheat, stirring often. The queso can be stored in an airtight container in the refrigerator for up to 3 days, but it's best the day it is made.

Creature Under the Stairs Tempura Green Bean "Fingers"

The Creature Under the Stairs has fingers like snakes, but he would surely venture out for these finger-like fried tempura green beans. The key to making sure your tempura stays crisp and not greasy is to keep the batter cold and your oil at the right temperature before frying. The fragrant dipping sauce is optional but well worth the effort.

Yield: 4 servings | Difficulty: Medium

FOR THE SOY-GINGER DIPPING SAUCE

- ⅓ cup water
- ¼ cup reduced-sodium soy sauce or tamari
- 2 tablespoons mirin (rice cooking wine)
- ½ teaspoon rice vinegar
- ½ teaspoon sugar
- ¼ teaspoon peeled and finely grated fresh ginger

FOR THE TEMPURA GREEN BEANS

- 1 cup ice-cold water
- 1 large egg
- ¾ cup plus 2 tablespoons all-purpose flour, sifted and divided
- 3 ice cubes
- Avocado or canola oil, for frying
- 1 pound fresh green beans, trimmed, washed, and dried
- Salt

TO MAKE THE SOY-GINGER DIPPING SAUCE

1. In a small saucepan over medium heat, whisk together the water, soy sauce, mirin, rice vinegar, sugar, and ginger. Stir until the sugar is dissolved and the mixture is fragrant. Pour into a bowl, and set aside.

TO MAKE THE TEMPURA GREEN BEANS

2. In a large bowl, whisk together the cold water and the egg. Sift the ¾ cup flour over the egg mixture, and whisk to combine; the batter will be lumpy. Add the ice cubes.

3. Line a large rimmed baking sheet with paper towels, and place it near the stove. Pour oil into a heavy saucepan or deep fryer to a depth of 2 inches. Set the pan over medium-high heat until the oil reaches 360°F on a deep-fry thermometer. Adjust the stovetop temperature as needed to maintain the correct temperature while frying.

4. Meanwhile, spread the green beans into an even layer on another large rimmed baking sheet. Dust with the remaining 2 tablespoons flour, tossing until evenly coated.

5. When the oil is ready, add one-third of the beans to the batter, submerging them to coat evenly. Using tongs, remove the green beans from the batter a few at a time, letting the excess batter drip back into the bowl. Carefully lower them into the hot oil. Fry, stirring occasionally with the tongs, until crisp and lightly browned, about 3 minutes.

6. Using the tongs, remove the beans from the pot and transfer to the paper-towel-lined plate to drain. Season with salt to taste. Repeat to cook the rest of the beans in the same way, making sure the oil returns to 360°F between batches.

TO SERVE

7. Place the bowl of dipping sauce on a serving plate and pile the tempura green beans around. Serve at once.

Starters & Sides

Oogie Boogie Bag of Bugs

Dr. Finkelstein Roasted Cauliflower "Brain" With Tomato Chutney

Snake and Spider Stew

Worm's Wort and Frog's Breath Soup

Roasted Jack-O'-Lantern Salad With Bloody Orange Vinaigrette

Harlequin Demon Sweet Potato Fries With Ranch Dressing

Full Moon Mashed Potatoes

Traditional multicourse dinners have just that—multiple courses—and the first is appropriately named the starter. Starters can be soups, salads, or exceptional vegetable dishes. However, unlike the soup Sally serves Dr. Finkelstein, they aren't intended to be eaten at the exclusion of the entrée.

Sides accompany the main dish, and there are no rules as to what you can offer—for instance, you can set out any starters as a side, too! Sides can be as complex as the Clown with the Tear-Away Face or as uncomplicated as the Creature Under the Bed. They can provide a counterpart to the entrée: Where one is spicy, the other can be mild; crunchy alongside tender; salty paired with sweet. Sides can also augment the theme of your dinner: Choose sides with the same color palette as the entrée, such as fiery oranges evocative of Halloween Town or the whites and reds of Christmas Town. You can even select the sides' colors so they evoke the red, green, and white faces of Lock, Shock, and Barrel!

Oogie Boogie Bag of Bugs

A big bowl of roasted brussels sprouts, earthy walnuts, and sweet-tart cranberries is a far better offering than a dish of Oogie Boogie bugs, even if they might resemble one another on a creepy Halloween-inspired spread. For the most flavor, select small, sweet sprouts in the fall or winter when they are in season.

Yield: 4 to 6 servings | Difficulty: Easy

- 2 pounds small brussels sprouts, trimmed and halved lengthwise
- 2 tablespoons extra-virgin olive oil
- Salt and freshly ground black pepper
- 2 tablespoons balsamic vinegar
- 1 tablespoon firmly packed light brown sugar
- ⅓ cup toasted walnuts, chopped
- ¼ cup dried cranberries

1. Preheat the oven to 400°F. On a large rimmed baking sheet, toss the brussels sprouts with olive oil until evenly coated. Season with salt and pepper, and toss again. Roast, stirring occasionally, until crisp-tender and browned, about 20 minutes.

2. Remove the baking sheet from the oven, and sprinkle the sprouts with the balsamic vinegar and brown sugar. Toss to coat evenly. Add the walnuts and cranberries, and toss to distribute evenly. Return the pan to the oven, and roast until the brussels sprouts are glazed, crisp, and tender, 3 to 5 minutes longer. Transfer to a serving bowl, and serve at once.

"Mister Oogie Boogie says there's trouble close at hand. You'd better pay attention now, 'cause I'm the Boogie Man."

—OOGIE BOOGIE

Dr. Finkelstein Roasted Cauliflower "Brain" With Tomato Chutney

Like a giant roasted brain, this whole cauliflower is a showstopper. It makes a terrific side dish or vegetarian main dish. A mix of spices adds warm flavor to the cauliflower, but don't forgo the tomato chutney—it's so good you might want to eat it on just about everything.

Yield: 6 servings | Difficulty: Easy

FOR THE ROASTED CAULIFLOWER

- 2 tablespoons avocado or canola oil
- 1 teaspoon garam masala
- ½ teaspoon ground turmeric
- ½ teaspoon ground cumin
- ½ teaspoon sweet paprika
- ¼ teaspoon ground ginger
- ½ teaspoon salt
- 1 head cauliflower (about 1½ pounds)

FOR THE TOMATO CHUTNEY

- 2 tablespoons avocado or canola oil
- 1 teaspoon whole yellow mustard seeds
- ½ cup finely chopped yellow onion
- 1 large clove garlic, minced
- ¼ cup firmly packed light brown sugar
- 3 tablespoons apple cider vinegar
- ¼ teaspoon ground cinnamon
- ¼ teaspoon ground ginger
- ½ teaspoon salt, plus more if needed
- One 14.5-ounce can crushed tomatoes
- 1 teaspoon lemon juice

1. Preheat the oven to 400°F. Place a 10-inch cast-iron pan on the middle rack in the oven. Place another small heatproof pan three-quarters full of water in the bottom of the oven.

TO MAKE THE ROASTED CAULIFLOWER

2. In a bowl, whisk together the avocado or canola oil, garam masala, turmeric, cumin, paprika, ginger, and salt. Rinse and dry the cauliflower. Trim away the leaves at the bottom of the head, then carefully cut out the core, leaving the florets and the cauliflower head intact. Brush the cauliflower all over with the spice paste.

3. Transfer the cauliflower to the hot cast-iron pan, placing it flat side down. Roast until browned and tender and a knife easily pierces the cauliflower, 45 to 50 minutes.

TO MAKE THE TOMATO CHUTNEY

4. While the cauliflower roasts, warm the avocado or canola oil in a saucepan over medium-low heat. Add the mustard seeds, onion, and garlic. Cook, stirring, until the onion softens, about 5 minutes. Stir in the sugar, vinegar, cinnamon, ginger, salt, and tomatoes. Simmer, stirring often, until the mixture thickens, about 15 minutes. Remove from the heat, and stir in the lemon juice. Season with more salt if needed. Let cool. The chutney can be made up to 1 week in advance and stored in an airtight container in the refrigerator.

TO SERVE

5. Transfer the cauliflower to a cutting board and cut into wedges. Serve wedges with the chutney.

Snake and Spider Stew

Oogie Boogie's favorite meal is Snake and Spider Stew! The noodles here are a slithery snake-like addition and add heartiness, but for a more traditional albondigas soup, omit the noodles.

Yield: 6 servings | Difficulty: Easy

FOR THE MEATBALLS

- ½ pound ground beef
- ½ pound ground pork
- 1 large egg
- ¼ cup fresh bread crumbs
- 2 tablespoons fresh cilantro, minced
- 1 clove garlic, minced
- ½ teaspoon ground cumin
- ½ teaspoon fine sea salt
- ¼ teaspoon freshly ground black pepper

FOR THE SOUP

- 2 tablespoons olive oil or avocado oil
- ½ medium yellow onion, finely chopped
- 2 medium carrots, peeled and diced
- 1 large celery stalk, diced
- Fine sea salt and freshly ground black pepper
- 2 cloves garlic, minced
- 1 teaspoon dried oregano, preferably Mexican
- 1 teaspoon ground cumin
- One 15-ounce can fire-roasted diced tomatoes
- 6 cups low-sodium chicken stock
- Sliced jalapeño (optional)
- 8 ounces ribbon pasta, such as fettuccine
- Juice of 1 lime, plus more to taste
- ¼ cup fresh cilantro, chopped

1. To make the meatballs, in a medium mixing bowl gently mix together the ground beef, ground pork, egg, bread crumbs, cilantro, garlic, cumin, salt, and pepper. Scoop tablespoonfuls of the dough and form into 1-inch-round meatballs. Transfer to a baking sheet.

2. In a Dutch oven over medium-high heat, warm the oil. Add the meatballs, turning once, until richly browned on two sides, about 5 minutes. Transfer to a plate.

3. Pour off all but 2 tablespoons of the fat. Add the onion, carrot, celery, and a pinch of salt to the Dutch oven. Cook over medium heat, stirring, until tender and golden, about 7 minutes. Add the garlic, oregano, cumin, ¼ teaspoon salt, and ¼ teaspoon pepper, and stir until fragrant, about 30 seconds. Stir in the diced tomatoes, then the chicken stock. Increase the heat to medium-high and bring to a boil. Reduce the heat to low and simmer for 15 minutes.

4. Bring a saucepan half full of salted water to a boil. Add the meatballs to the soup and simmer over low heat, stirring occasionally, until cooked through, about 10 minutes. Add the pasta to the boiling water and cook until just al dente, according to package directions. Drain and add to the soup. Stir in the lime juice. Taste and adjust the seasoning.

5. Divide between shallow bowls, garnish with the cilantro, and serve at once.

Worm's Wort and Frog's Breath Soup

To secure her freedom from Dr. Finkelstein, Sally cooks up a cauldron of Deadly Nightshade soup, masked with the flavors of worm's wort and frog's breath. This soup is made with much friendlier ingredients without the poisonous side effects. You won't need your slotted spoons for serving this fresh and creamy soup.

Yield: 4 to 6 servings (about 6 cups soup) | Difficulty: Easy

- 2 tablespoons unsalted butter
- 2 leeks, white and light green parts, finely chopped
- ½ teaspoon salt, plus more to taste
- 1 medium russet potato (8 to 10 ounces), peeled and cut into 1-inch chunks
- 4 cups low-sodium vegetable or chicken broth, plus more if needed
- 1 pound medium-thin asparagus, trimmed and cut into 1½-inch pieces
- Freshly ground black pepper
- 2 tablespoons heavy cream, for serving (optional)
- 1 tablespoon fresh chives, finely chopped, for garnish

1. In a large saucepan over medium heat, melt the butter. Add the leeks and ½ teaspoon salt, and cook, stirring occasionally, until softened but not browned, about 5 minutes. Add the potato and broth, increase the heat to medium-high, and bring to a boil. Reduce the heat to medium-low, and simmer, stirring occasionally, until the potato is tender, about 10 minutes. Add the asparagus, increase the heat to medium, and gently boil until the asparagus are just tender, about 5 minutes.

2. Working in batches, process the soup in a blender to a very smooth puree, then return to the pot. Season with salt and pepper, and thin with additional broth as needed. Reheat gently over low heat until warm. Ladle into individual bowls. Garnish with a drizzle of cream, if using, and chives. Serve.

Roasted Jack-O'-Lantern Salad With Bloody Orange Vinaigrette

Known as the Pumpkin King, Jack Skellington is the one who annually returns to the real world to scare young and old alike. You won't need to set anything ablaze with a burning torch to cook the pumpkin for this dish—just roast it in the oven.

Yield: 4 to 6 servings (about ⅔ cup dressing) | Difficulty: Easy

FOR THE BLOODY ORANGE VINAIGRETTE

- 1 blood orange
- 1 lemon
- 1 teaspoon Dijon mustard
- 1 teaspoon minced shallots
- Salt and freshly ground black pepper
- ½ cup extra-virgin olive oil

FOR THE ROASTED JACK-O'-LANTERN SALAD

- 1 small sugar pie pumpkin (2 pounds) or butternut squash (1½ pounds), peeled, halved, seeded, and cut into ¾-inch chunks
- 2 tablespoons olive oil
- Salt and freshly ground black pepper
- 1 tablespoon honey
- 6 thick slices (8 ounces) applewood-smoked bacon, chopped
- 10 ounces baby spinach
- ⅓ cup feta cheese, crumbled
- ¼ cup pepitas, toasted

TO MAKE THE VINAIGRETTE

1. Juice the blood orange and lemon into a glass jar; you should have a ½ cup of juice. Add the mustard, shallots, and a pinch of salt and pepper. Screw on the lid, and shake vigorously to combine. Add the oil, screw on the lid, and shake vigorously until emulsified. Season with additional salt and pepper if needed. Set aside while you make the salad.

TO MAKE THE SALAD

2. Preheat the oven to 450°F. Place the pumpkin on a baking sheet and drizzle with the olive oil, then season with salt and pepper. Toss until evenly coated, then spread into an even layer. Roast, stirring once halfway through, until tender and browned, about 15 minutes. Drizzle with the honey, stir to combine, and continue to roast until glazed, 1 to 2 minutes longer. Set aside to cool.

3. In a frying pan over medium-low heat, cook the bacon, stirring occasionally, until crisp and browned, about 8 minutes. Using a slotted spoon, transfer to paper towels to drain.

TO ASSEMBLE THE SALAD

4. Put the spinach, bacon, and roasted pumpkin in a wide salad bowl. Drizzle with ¼ cup vinaigrette, and toss to combine. Garnish with the feta and pepitas. Serve the salad, passing additional vinaigrette alongside.

Harlequin Demon Sweet Potato Fries With Ranch Dressing

With his black and orange tentacles and enormous mouth of sharp teeth, the Harlequin Demon is nothing short of scary. But we think even these sweet potato tentacle fries would give him a toothy grin, especially when served with a creamy homemade ranch dip.

Yield: 4 to 6 servings | Difficulty: Easy

FOR THE RANCH DRESSING

- ½ cup mayonnaise
- ½ cup buttermilk
- 1 teaspoon fresh flat-leaf parsley, minced
- 1 teaspoon fresh chives, minced
- 1 teaspoon fresh dill, minced
- ½ teaspoon onion powder
- ½ teaspoon garlic powder
- ½ teaspoon salt
- ¼ teaspoon freshly ground black pepper

FOR THE SWEET POTATO FRIES

- 2 pounds sweet potatoes
- 2 tablespoons olive oil
- Salt and freshly ground black pepper

TIP

For the crispiest fries, be sure to spread out the sweet potato batons so they aren't touching on the baking sheet.

TO MAKE THE RANCH DRESSING

1. In a bowl, whisk together the mayonnaise, buttermilk, parsley, chives, dill, onion powder, garlic powder, salt, and pepper. Taste and adjust the seasonings. Cover and store in the refrigerator until ready to use or for up to 3 days.

TO MAKE THE SWEET POTATO FRIES

2. Preheat the oven to 450°F. Trim the ends of the sweet potatoes, then cut lengthwise into ½-inch slices. Cut each slice into batons that are about ¼-inch wide.

3. Transfer the sweet potatoes to a large rimmed baking sheet. Toss with the olive oil until coated evenly. Spread into an even layer. Roast, stirring once, until tender and browned on the edges, 20 to 25 minutes. Season with salt and pepper. Pile on a plate with the bowl of ranch dressing alongside for dipping.

Full Moon Mashed Potatoes

For this dish, it's all about the assembly to create a scene straight out of the movie. Warm a platter by pouring boiling water over it in the sink. Make sure it's big enough to spread out the cabbage on one half so it looks like the pumpkin patch, and then scoop the potatoes into a big round to resemble the full moon. A little mountain swirl of cabbage atop the potatoes finishes the effect.

Yield: 6 to 8 servings | Difficulty: Easy

FOR THE BRAISED RED CABBAGE
- 3 tablespoons extra-virgin olive oil
- 1 small yellow onion, thinly sliced
- Salt and freshly ground black pepper
- 1 head red cabbage, about 2 pounds, cored and finely shredded
- 1 tart green apple such as Granny Smith, halved, cored, and thinly sliced
- ¼ cup balsamic vinegar

FOR THE MASHED POTATOES
- 3 pounds Yukon gold potatoes, peeled and cut into 1-inch chunks
- 1 tablespoon plus ½ teaspoon salt
- 6 tablespoons (¾ stick) butter, at room temperature, sliced
- ¾ cup whole milk, warmed
- ¼ teaspoon freshly ground white pepper

TO MAKE THE CABBAGE

1. In a large saucepan over medium heat, warm the olive oil. Add the onion and a pinch of salt, and cook, stirring occasionally, until the onion is soft and translucent, about 5 minutes. Add the cabbage and apple slices, and stir to combine. Add the vinegar and ½ cup water, and season with salt and pepper. Bring the liquid to a boil. Reduce the heat to low, partially cover the pan, and simmer, stirring occasionally, until the cabbage is tender, about 30 minutes. Uncover and continue to simmer gently until most of the liquid has evaporated, about 15 minutes longer.

TO MAKE THE MASHED POTATOES

2. While the cabbage cooks, add the potatoes to a large saucepan, and add enough water to cover. Add 1 tablespoon salt. Bring to a boil over high heat. Reduce the heat to medium-low, and simmer, stirring occasionally, until the potatoes are tender when pierced with a knife, about 20 minutes. Drain well and return to the saucepan. Use a potato masher to roughly mash the potatoes. Add the butter, milk, remaining ½ teaspoon salt, and the white pepper to the potatoes. Using a handheld mixer fitted with the beater attachment, beat the potatoes until smooth, or to the desired texture. Be careful not to overbeat the potatoes. Season with more salt and pepper if needed. Cover to keep warm.

3. When ready to serve, spread all but 1 cup of the cabbage on half of a warm serving platter. Pile the potatoes on the other half in a large, thick round disk, to look like a full moon over the pumpkin patch. Use the remaining 1 cup cabbage to create a swirled mountain silhouette across the bottom of the potato moon. Serve at once.

3

Entrées

Behemoth BBQ Pork Buns

Cyclops Eye Stuffed Chicken Shawarma Mini Pitas

Oogie Boogie Pasta Worms

Roasted Squash Mummy Tartlets

Mummy Boy Dogs

Christmas Tree Veggie Pizza With Spiders

Clown With the Tear-Away Face Pepperoni Pizza

Full Moon Spanish Tortilla

Sally Cauldron Potpies

Jack Skellington Shepherd's Pie

Christmas Tree Empanadas

Man-Eating Wreath Burritos

Zero Barbecued Ribs

Jack Skellington Cheese and Veggie Quesadillas

The entrées in this section provide a variety of tastes for any occasion no matter what Holiday Door you choose to step through. Many of the recipes take advantage of seasonal vegetables, while hot dogs and barbecued ribs epitomize summer celebrations. But of course, any and all of these can be served year-round for any holiday or get-together.

Each of these dishes offers a tasty visual nod to Halloween Town or Christmas Town, depicting full moons, wrapped mummies, decorated holiday trees, and sometimes a mish-mash-up of both. Whether savory or spicy, as Sally would say, they're scrumptious!

Behemoth BBQ Pork Buns

Behemoth's round, squishy head looks an awful lot like a fluffy steamed pork bun. Forming the buns takes a little practice, so take your time when pleating. The roasted pork filling is also excellent on its own, served over steamed jasmine rice.

Yield: 15 buns | Difficulty: Hard

FOR THE BBQ PORK FILLING

- 5 tablespoons hoisin sauce
- 3 tablespoons reduced-sodium soy sauce
- 2 tablespoons honey
- 2 tablespoons rice wine, such as Shaoxing or mirin
- 2 teaspoons toasted sesame oil
- ½ teaspoon Chinese five-spice powder
- ¼ teaspoon freshly ground black pepper
- 2 cloves garlic, peeled and crushed
- 8 to 10 ounces boneless pork shoulder steak, trimmed of excess fat

FOR THE DOUGH (ABOUT 1½ POUNDS)

- 1½ cups all-purpose flour
- 1½ cups cake flour
- 3 tablespoons sugar
- 2 teaspoons baking powder
- ½ teaspoon salt
- 1 cup warm (110°F) water
- 2 tablespoons avocado or canola oil
- 1½ teaspoons instant yeast

FOR THE SAUCE

- 1 tablespoon rice vinegar
- 1½ teaspoons cornstarch
- 1 tablespoon avocado or canola oil
- 3 small green onions, white and green parts, thinly sliced
- 2 teaspoons peeled and grated fresh ginger

TO MAKE THE FILLING

1. In a bowl, whisk together the hoisin sauce, soy sauce, honey, rice wine, sesame oil, five-spice, and black pepper. Add ¼ cup of the mixture to a baking dish just large enough to hold the pork shoulder in a single layer, and add the garlic. Add the pork, and turn to coat. Cover and refrigerate for at least 4 hours but ideally overnight. Cover the remaining marinade (you should have ½ cup), and refrigerate until ready to make the buns. Remove the pork from the refrigerator an hour before cooking.

TO MAKE THE DOUGH

2. In the bowl of a stand mixer fitted with the dough hook, whisk together the all-purpose flour, cake flour, sugar, baking powder, and salt. In a small bowl, whisk together the water, oil, and yeast. Add the yeast mixture to the flour mixture, and mix on medium speed until the dough is smooth and feels like a marshmallow, about 10 minutes. Form the dough into a ball and place in a lightly oiled bowl. Cover with a damp kitchen towel, and set aside in a warm, draft-free place until doubled in size, about 1½ hours.

TO MAKE THE PORK

3. While the dough rises, preheat the oven to 450°F. Line a rimmed baking sheet or shallow roasting pan with aluminum foil, and position a rack inside or on top. Remove the pork from the marinade, letting the excess drip back into the bowl, and arrange the pork on the rack.

4. Roast the pork, turning once halfway through, until charred and cooked through, about 30 minutes. Transfer the pork to a cutting board, and let rest for 15 minutes. Slice the meat thinly, then chop into small ½-inch pieces. Transfer to a bowl. Set aside.

TO MAKE THE SAUCE

5. In a small bowl, whisk together the vinegar and cornstarch. In a small frying pan, warm the oil over medium heat. Add the green onions and ginger, and cook, stirring, until wilted, about 30 seconds. Add the ½ cup reserved marinade, and cook until warmed, about 1 minute. Add the cornstarch mixture, and simmer until a silky sauce forms, about 1 minute. Pour the sauce over the reserved pork, stirring to combine.

TO ASSEMBLE

6. Cut fifteen 3-inch squares out of parchment paper. Turn the dough out onto a lightly floured work surface. Divide the dough into fifteen pieces, each about 1½ ounces (a kitchen scale works well for this). Roll each piece of dough into a ball; cover the dough balls with a damp cloth while you roll them to keep a skin from forming. On a lightly floured surface, starting with the first ball you rolled, roll the dough into a 4½-inch round. Use your thumbs and forefingers to pinch around the edge so it is thinner than the center. Holding the dough round cupped in the palm of your hand, place 1 tablespoon of the pork filling into the center. Use your cupped hand to help push up the dough edges and pleat, pinch, and twist the edge up to completely enclose the filling. Place the bun on a parchment square, then place on a large rimmed baking sheet. Cover loosely with plastic wrap while you continue forming the buns.

7. Prepare a stovetop steamer. Starting with the buns you assembled first, add as many buns as you can to the steamer, while keeping them spaced about 1 inch apart. Steam until puffed and dry-looking but still white, 13 to 15 minutes. Transfer to a warm platter, and repeat to cook all the buns. Leftover buns can be stored in an airtight container in the refrigerator for up to 1 week; steam before serving.

Cyclops Eye Stuffed Chicken Shawarma Mini Pitas

The large yellow eye of the Cyclops looks just like a round mini pita. You can assemble all the sandwiches and serve them on a platter, or put out bowls of the ingredients alongside the split, warmed pita and invite guests to create their own Cyclops-eye pitas.

Yield: 4 to 6 servings | Difficulty: Easy

FOR THE TAHINI-LEMON SAUCE

- ¼ cup tahini
- ¼ cup fresh lemon juice
- 2 tablespoons plain yogurt
- 1 tablespoon olive oil
- ¼ teaspoon salt

FOR THE MEDITERRANEAN SALAD

- 1 cup fresh tomatoes, diced, or cherry tomatoes, quartered
- ½ cup English cucumber, diced
- 2 tablespoons fresh flat-leaf parsley, finely chopped
- 1 tablespoon extra-virgin olive oil
- Salt and freshly ground black pepper

FOR THE CHICKEN SHAWARMA

- 3 tablespoons olive oil
- 2 tablespoons fresh lemon juice
- 1 teaspoon ground cumin
- 1 teaspoon sweet paprika
- 2 cloves garlic, minced
- ½ teaspoon salt
- ¼ teaspoon freshly ground black pepper
- ¾ to 1 pound boneless, skinless chicken breast halves, cut crosswise into ½-inch-thick strips
- ½ red onion, thinly sliced
- 8 to 10 mini pita breads, warmed

TO MAKE THE SAUCE

1. In a bowl, whisk together the tahini, lemon juice, yogurt, olive oil, and salt. Cover and refrigerate until ready to use, up to 2 days in advance.

TO MAKE THE SALAD

2. In a medium bowl, toss together the tomatoes, cucumber, and parsley. Drizzle with the olive oil, and season with salt and pepper. Toss to combine. Set aside at room temperature.

TO MAKE THE CHICKEN

3. In a large bowl, stir together 1 tablespoon of the olive oil, the lemon juice, cumin, paprika, garlic, salt, and pepper. Add the chicken, and toss until well coated. Let stand at room temperature for 20 minutes or refrigerate for up to 1 day (if refrigerated, let stand at room temperature for 15 minutes).

4. Heat a large cast-iron pan over medium-high heat. Add 1 tablespoon of the olive oil to the pan, then add the onion, spreading it in an even layer. Cook, turning occasionally with tongs, until nicely browned on both sides, about 4 minutes. Transfer to a plate.

5. Add the remaining 1 tablespoon of olive oil. Add the chicken strips to the pan, spreading them in an even layer, and cook, turning once, until lightly browned on both sides and opaque throughout, about 3 minutes on each side. Transfer the chicken to the plate with the onions.

TO ASSEMBLE

6. Carefully cut open the pita halves to create pockets. Fill each pocket with the grilled chicken mixture and the salad, dividing the fillings evenly. Generously drizzle the fillings in each pita with the tahini sauce. Arrange the pitas on a platter. Serve at once.

Oogie Boogie Pasta Worms

Filled with insects, spiders, and plenty of worms, Oogie Boogie is a terrifying creature bent on destroying Santa Claus. But this big bowl of wormlike pasta is anything but terrifying. Bucatini is a long, thick pasta with a hollow center, but spaghetti or linguine can easily be substituted.

Yield: 4 to 6 servings | Difficulty: Easy

- 2 tablespoons extra-virgin olive oil
- 4 ounces pancetta or bacon, chopped
- 1 small yellow onion, finely chopped
- 3 cloves garlic, minced
- ½ teaspoon red pepper flakes (optional)
- One 28-ounce can crushed tomatoes

- ½ teaspoon dried oregano
- Salt and freshly ground black pepper
- 1 pound bucatini or spaghetti
- ¼ cup Parmesan cheese, grated
- 2 tablespoons finely chopped fresh basil

1. In a large saucepan over medium-high heat, warm the olive oil. Add the pancetta and cook, stirring occasionally, until the pancetta is crisp and browned, about 5 minutes. Add the onion and cook, stirring occasionally, until translucent, about 6 minutes. Add the garlic and red pepper flakes, if using, and cook until the garlic softens, 1 to 2 minutes. Add the tomatoes, stir to combine, and bring to a boil. Reduce the heat to low, stir in the oregano, and simmer, stirring occasionally, to blend the flavors, about 15 minutes. Season with salt and pepper. Cover to keep warm, and set aside.

2. While the sauce simmers, fill a large pot three-quarters full of water. Bring to a boil over high heat. Add 1 tablespoon salt and the bucatini, stir well, and cook until the pasta is al dente, about 10 minutes or according to package directions. Drain the pasta in a fine mesh sieve.

3. Rewarm the sauce on the stove, then transfer the pasta to the pot of sauce. Using tongs, toss the pasta and sauce until the pasta is evenly coated. Add half the Parmesan and toss again. Transfer to a wide serving bowl. Sprinkle the pasta with the remaining cheese and the basil, and serve right away.

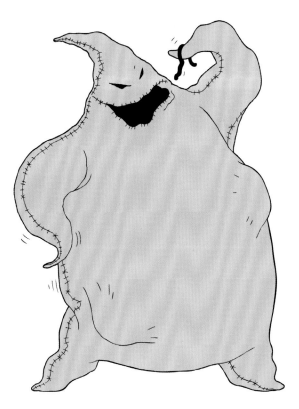

Roasted Squash Mummy Tartlets

These mummy tartlets are stuffed with sweet roasted butternut squash and salty goat cheese and topped with olive eyes. You can use other winter squash, like kuri, kabocha, or sugar pie pumpkin, or swap out the goat cheese for feta if you like. This technique can be used with other fillings such as apple or peach for a sweet treat. Make sure to thaw the puff pastry before you get started, ideally overnight in the refrigerator.

Yield: 9 tartlets | Difficulty: Medium

- 1 small butternut squash (about 1½ pounds), peeled, halved lengthwise, seeded, and cut into ½-inch chunks
- 1 tablespoon olive oil
- Salt and freshly ground black pepper
- One 17-ounce package frozen puff pastry sheets, thawed

- 1 large egg, beaten with 1 teaspoon water, for egg wash
- 4 ounces fresh goat cheese, crumbled
- 9 black olives, sliced

1. Preheat the oven to 425°F. Place the squash on a baking sheet, and drizzle with 1 tablespoon olive oil, then season with salt and pepper. Toss until evenly coated, then spread into an even layer. Roast until just tender and lightly browned, about 25 minutes. Transfer to a medium bowl, and mash the squash with a fork. Let cool completely.

2. Reduce the oven temperature to 400°F. Line the baking sheet with parchment paper. On a lightly floured surface, roll out one sheet of puff pastry into a 13-inch square. Using a 4-inch-round cutter (or a bowl of the same size and a sharp paring knife), cut out nine rounds. Transfer the rounds to the baking sheet.

3. Brush the top side of each round lightly with the egg wash. Divide the mashed squash evenly over the pastry rounds, leaving a ½-inch border all the way around. Top the squash with the goat cheese in an even layer. Place one olive slice on top of each round for the mummy eye.

4. Roll out the remaining puff pastry into a 13-inch square. Using a pizza cutter, cut the pastry crosswise into thin ½-inch strips. Using the 4-inch cutter, cut out nine rounds of the strips. Brush the pastry strips with the egg wash. Arrange the strips over the tops of the tarts, egg wash side down, placing them at angles over the filling, and covering the filling entirely but leaving the olive eye exposed, so they look like mummies. Press the edges down to adhere to the bottom pastry round. Place the baking sheet in the refrigerator for 30 minutes for the tartlets to chill.

5. Bake the tartlets until the puff pastry is crisp and golden brown, 25 to 30 minutes. Let cool slightly, then serve while warm.

Mummy Boy Dogs

Kids will scream with delight when served these pastry-wrapped hot dogs. You can swap in any kind of precooked sausage, as long as they are all about the right length. Using store-bought puff pastry makes this easy, but you can also use pie dough cut into strips as directed. If black olives are a no-go, you can make the mummy eyes with a dot of ketchup or mustard instead.

Yield: 6 servings | Difficulty: Easy

- One 8-ounce sheet frozen puff pastry, thawed
- 1 large egg, beaten with 1 teaspoon water, for egg wash
- 6 hot dogs or smoked sausages, each 5 to 6 inches long
- 6 small black olives, sliced
- Ketchup and/or mustard, for serving

1. Line a large rimmed baking sheet with parchment paper. On a lightly floured work surface, roll out the puff pastry to a ⅛-inch thick rectangle about 12 inches long and 9 inches wide. Using a pizza cutter, cut ½-inch-wide strips along the long side of the pastry. You should end up with 18 strips.

2. Using 3 strips per hot dog, dip the ends of the pastry into the egg wash and wrap them around each hot dog, leaving a small slit near the top of each sausage for the "eye." Tuck one black olive slice near the top for the eye. Place the wrapped hot dogs on the prepared baking sheet, spacing them apart. Refrigerate for 15 minutes.

3. Preheat the oven to 400°F. Lightly brush the pastry-wrapped hot dogs all over with the egg wash. Bake until puffed and golden brown, about 22 minutes. Serve at once with ketchup or mustard alongside for dipping.

Christmas Tree Veggie Pizza With Spiders

This Christmas-tree-shaped veggie pizza couldn't be cuter, until it gets a Halloween Town makeover with plenty of creepy spiders crawling across its branches. Let the dough rest for a few minutes if it becomes difficult to roll or shape.

Yield: 2 to 4 servings (1 large pizza) | Difficulty: Medium

- 1 pound store-bought refrigerated pizza dough, at room temperature
- Cornmeal, for dusting
- ⅓ cup store-bought pesto sauce
- Olive oil

- 3 ounces mozzarella cheese, shredded
- 8 black olives, pitted
- ½ fresh red bell pepper, roughly chopped
- 2 or 3 thin slices red onion, halved

1. If you have a pizza stone, set it on a rack in the lower third of the oven. About 30 minutes before you want to make the pizza, preheat the oven to 450°F. Sprinkle cornmeal over a pizza peel or the flat side of a rimless baking sheet to prepare.

2. Pull off a small piece of dough and shape into a small rectangle for the trunk of the tree. Gently pull the remaining dough into a long triangle, or use a rolling pin to roll it out; if the dough springs back, let it rest for 5 or 10 minutes before proceeding. Slide the dough onto the peel or rimless baking sheet, and press the rectangle onto the bottom of the triangle-shaped tree to resemble a trunk.

3. Spread the pesto evenly over the dough all the way to the edge but not on the trunk. Brush the trunk with the olive oil. Scatter the cheese in an even layer over the pesto. Arrange the red onion slices to look like garlands on the tree and the red bell pepper pieces to look like ornaments. To make "spiders," cut four olives in half lengthwise. Place the olive halves, cut side down, onto the pizza, spacing them around the pizza evenly; these are the spider bodies. Cut the remaining four olives in half. Cut each half lengthwise into eight thin slivers to create eight legs per spider. Arrange eight legs around each spider body on the pizza.

4. If using a pizza stone, gently shake the peel to loosen the pizza. Place the rounded end of the peel over the far side of the pizza stone. Tip the peel to allow the pizza to fall onto the stone while slipping the peel from underneath the pizza. If you are using the baking sheet, simply place the pan in the lower third of the oven. Bake until the bottom of the crust is crisp and the top is bubbling, about 10 minutes.

5. Transfer the pizza to a cutting board. Slice and serve while the pizza is hot.

Clown With the Tear-Away Face Pepperoni Pizza

Pizza is the perfect party food, and a pizza-making party is a great way to engage kids and adults alike in working together in the kitchen, especially when re-creating the Clown with the Tear-Away Face's frightening toothy grin out of pepperoni! Be sure to preheat the oven until it's extra hot, that way the pizza puffs nicely and browns quickly

Yield: 2 to 4 servings (1 large pizza) | Difficulty: Easy

- 1 pound store-bought refrigerated pizza dough, at room temperature
- Cornmeal, for dusting
- Olive oil

- ½ cup store-bought pizza sauce
- 1 cup shredded mozzarella cheese
- 10 to 12 thinly sliced pepperoni (about 1½ ounces)

1. If you have a pizza stone, set it on a rack in the lower third of the oven. About 30 minutes before you want to make the pizza, preheat the oven to 450°F. Sprinkle cornmeal over a pizza peel or the flat side of a rimless baking sheet to prepare.

2. Gently pull the dough into a 12-inch round, or use a rolling pin to roll it out; if the dough springs back, let it rest for 5 or 10 minutes before proceeding. Gently slide the dough round onto the peel or baking sheet.

3. Brush the edge of the pizza dough lightly with olive oil. Spread the pizza sauce evenly over the dough, to within ½ inch of the edge, then scatter with the cheese in an even layer. Arrange the pepperoni on top to look like the Clown with the Tear-Away Face: Use two pepperoni slices as eyes and one as a nose. Cut the remaining into quarters and create a toothy grin, angry eyebrows, and the top of his beanie hat. Alternatively, arrange the slices so they look like polka dots all over the pizza.

4. If using a pizza stone, gently shake the peel to loosen the pizza. Place the rounded end of the peel over the far side of the pizza stone. Tip the peel to allow the pizza to fall onto the stone while slipping the peel from underneath the pizza. If you are using the baking sheet, simply place the pan in the lower third of the oven. Bake until the bottom of the crust is crisp and the top is blistered, about 10 minutes.

5. Transfer the pizza to a cutting board. Slice and serve while the pizza is hot.

Full Moon Spanish Tortilla

This vegetarian entrée is more like a frittata—heavy on the potatoes—and less like flatbread. The golden color and crater-like ridges make it look like a big beautiful moon rising over the mountain. It's great for a party, because it can be served at room temperature and cut into bite-sized pieces for an easy starter.

Yield: 6 servings | Difficulty: Medium

- 2 pounds russet potatoes (about 3 large), peeled, halved lengthwise, and sliced crosswise, ⅛-inch thick
- 2 medium yellow onions, peeled, halved lengthwise, and sliced crosswise, ¼-inch thick

- 1 cup olive oil
- 3 large eggs
- 1 teaspoon salt
- ½ teaspoon freshly ground black pepper

1. Add the cut potatoes to a large bowl half full of cold water. Set aside.

2. In a large nonstick frying pan over medium heat, combine the onions with the olive oil. Cook, stirring, until the onions are translucent and tender, about 10 minutes. Drain the potatoes in a large fine-mesh sieve, shaking off as much excess water as possible, then add them to the frying pan. Cook, stirring occasionally and moving the mixture around so the potatoes cook evenly, until tender but still holding their shape, about 15 minutes.

3. Set the fine-mesh sieve into the bowl the potatoes were in. Drain the potatoes and onions in the sieve. Transfer the olive oil to another bowl. In the large bowl, whisk together the eggs, salt, and pepper. Add the potato mixture and gently but quickly stir the mixture together to incorporate the egg.

4. Return the frying pan to medium heat, and add 2 tablespoons reserved olive oil. Swirl it around, then add the potato mixture. Using the back of a spatula, flatten the potato mixture out into a thick round, smoothing the edges. Cook, gently shaking the pan back and forth to keep the tortilla from sticking, until the bottom is golden brown, about 5 minutes.

5. Invert a large plate over the top of the tortilla and then invert the pan and tortilla onto the plate. Put the pan back over medium heat. (If there are bits that stick to the pan, add them back to the tortilla and clean out the pan.) Add 2 tablespoons of reserved olive oil, swirl the pan, and slide the tortilla, uncooked side down, into the pan. Use the spatula to re-form the tortilla into a thick round.

6. Cook, gently shaking the pan back and forth to keep the tortilla from sticking, until the bottom is golden brown and the tortilla is cooked through, about 5 minutes longer. Invert the large plate over the top of the tortilla, and then invert the pan and tortilla onto the plate. Serve hot, warm, or at room temperature.

Sally Cauldron Potpies

Sally has a real talent for creating potions in her cauldron. Hone your talent with this recipe for mini-cauldron potpies filled with hearty vegetable stew. Make sure not to precook the vegetables too much, as they will continue to cook when the pies are baked.

Yield: 6 potpies | Difficulty: Medium

FOR THE FLAKY PIE DOUGH (SINGLE CRUST)

- 1½ cups all-purpose flour
- ¼ teaspoon salt
- 8 tablespoons (1 stick) very cold unsalted butter, cut into cubes
- 6 tablespoons ice-cold water, plus more if needed

FOR THE PIE FILLING

- 1 tablespoon plus ¾ teaspoon salt
- 4 cups (12 ounces) broccoli florets, cut into bite-sized pieces
- 7 tablespoons unsalted butter, divided
- 12 ounces cremini or button mushrooms, trimmed and sliced

- 2 medium carrots, peeled and finely diced
- 1 large leek, trimmed, halved lengthwise, and white and pale green parts thinly sliced
- 1 large stalk celery, finely chopped
- 2 teaspoons minced fresh thyme or oregano leaves
- ½ cup frozen peas
- ⅓ cup all-purpose flour
- 2 cups reduced-sodium vegetable or chicken broth
- 1 cup whole milk
- ¼ teaspoon freshly ground black pepper
- 1 large egg, beaten with 1 teaspoon water, for egg wash

TO MAKE THE PIE DOUGH

1. In the bowl of a food processor, pulse together the flour and salt. Sprinkle the butter over the top, and pulse until the butter is in pieces the size of small peas. Evenly sprinkle the water over the flour mixture, then process until the mixture starts to come together. Turn the dough onto a work surface, press it together into a disk, then wrap in plastic. Refrigerate the dough for 30 minutes or up to 1 day, or freeze for up to 1 month.

TO MAKE THE FILLING

2. Fill a medium saucepan halfway with water, and add 1 tablespoon salt. Bring to a boil over medium-high heat. Add the broccoli and cook for 1 minute. Drain and rinse under cold water to stop the cooking; drain well. Set aside.

3. In a large frying pan over medium heat, melt 2 tablespoons butter. Add the mushrooms, carrots, leek, celery, thyme, and ¼ teaspoon salt, and cook, stirring, until the vegetables are crisp-tender, about 5 minutes. Transfer to a large bowl, and stir in the broccoli and peas. Set aside to cool.

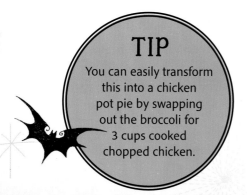

TIP

You can easily transform this into a chicken pot pie by swapping out the broccoli for 3 cups cooked chopped chicken.

4. In the frying pan over medium-low heat, melt the remaining 5 tablespoons butter. Whisk in the flour, and let bubble gently for 1 minute. Gradually whisk in the broth, then the milk. Increase the heat to medium, and bring to a boil, whisking frequently, then reduce the heat to medium-low, and simmer until slightly thickened, about 3 minutes. Season with remaining ½ teaspoon salt and ¼ teaspoon pepper, plus more if needed. Set aside to cool to room temperature.

5. While the vegetables and sauce cool, line a large rimmed baking sheet with parchment paper. On a lightly floured work surface, roll out the dough into a ⅛-inch-thick round. Using a 6-inch saucer as a template, use a paring knife to cut out six rounds (gather the scraps, press together, and reroll once). Transfer to the baking sheet, and refrigerate until ready to use.

6. Preheat the oven to 400°F. Add the sauce to the vegetable mixture, and stir to combine. Divide the mixture between six 1-cup (or four 1½-cup) ramekins or ovenproof baking dishes.

7. Place one dough round over each ramekin, gently pressing the dough around the ramekin edges. Place the ramekins on the prepared baking sheet. Lightly brush the dough with the egg wash.

8. Bake until the pastry is golden brown and the filling is bubbling, about 30 minutes. Transfer each ramekin to a plate and serve.

Jack Skellington Shepherd's Pie

A sea of fluffy mashed potatoes atop a robust lamb stew is a great canvas for showcasing Jack Skellington's iconic visage. Many versions of shepherd's pie exist, and while it is often made from ground lamb or beef, we love this braised version, which is perfect for a winter's night to ward off the ghoulish cold.

Yield: 6 servings | Difficulty: Easy

- 2 pounds boneless lamb shoulder or boneless beef chuck roast, trimmed of excess fat and cut into 1-inch pieces
- Salt and freshly ground black pepper
- 2 tablespoons olive oil
- 8 tablespoons (1 stick) butter, divided
- 1 yellow onion, finely chopped
- 3 carrots, peeled and finely diced
- 3 stalks celery, finely chopped
- 2 small cloves garlic, minced
- 6 tablespoons all-purpose flour
- 3⅓ cups beef stock
- ⅔ cup dry red wine
- 1 teaspoon minced fresh rosemary or thyme leaves
- 3 pounds russet potatoes, peeled and cut into chunks
- ⅓ cup heavy cream, warmed
- 1 cup fresh or thawed frozen peas

1. Preheat the oven to 325°F. Season the meat with salt and pepper. In a Dutch oven over medium-high heat, warm the olive oil. In batches to avoid crowding, add the meat, and cook, turning once, until browned on two sides, about 5 minutes per batch. Transfer to a plate.

2. Add 4 tablespoons of the butter to the Dutch oven and melt over medium heat. Add the onion, carrots, celery, and garlic, cover, and cook, stirring occasionally, until the vegetables are tender-crisp, about 5 minutes. Uncover, sprinkle with the flour, and stir well. Gradually stir in the stock and wine and then the rosemary. Bring to a boil over medium heat, stirring frequently. Return the meat to the Dutch oven, cover, and place in the oven. Cook, stirring occasionally, until the meat is tender, about 1½ hours.

3. About 30 minutes before the meat is ready, grease a round 3-quart baking dish. In a saucepan, combine the potatoes with salted water to cover, cover the pan, and bring to a boil over high heat. Uncover, reduce the heat to medium, and simmer until the potatoes are tender, 20 to 25 minutes. Drain well. Return the potatoes to the pan.

4. Cut 3 tablespoons of the butter into pieces, and add to the potatoes. Using a potato masher, mash the potatoes while adding the heavy cream to create a smooth mixture. Season with salt and pepper.

5. Season the meat mixture with salt and pepper, stir in the peas, and pour into the prepared baking dish. Spread the mashed potatoes evenly on top. Use a spoon to scoop out two rounds for Jack Skellington's eyes, then create a long wide Jack Skellington smile in the mashed potatoes. Cut the remaining 1 tablespoon of butter into small pieces and use it to dot the top of the potatoes. Bake in the 325° oven until the top is lightly browned, about 20 minutes. Remove from the oven, and let stand for about 5 minutes. If the potatoes have filled in the eyes and mouth, use a spoon to reshape them. Serve hot.

Christmas Tree Empanadas

Christmas-tree-shaped empanadas filled with savory-sweet beef picadillo are a delicious addition to your Christmas Town party during the holidays. You can bring a little Halloween Town into play by cutting out the flaky pastries as jack-o'-lanterns, or even circle shapes like Jack Skellington's head.

Yield: About 10 empanadas | Difficulty: Medium

FOR THE EMPANADA DOUGH

- 2½ cups all-purpose flour, plus more for dusting
- ½ teaspoon salt
- 10 tablespoons (1¼ stick) cold unsalted butter, cut into ½-inch cubes
- 1 large egg, lightly beaten
- 4 tablespoons ice-cold water, plus more if needed
- 1 tablespoon fresh lemon juice

FOR THE PICADILLO FILLING

- 2 tablespoons dried currants or raisins
- ½ cup boiling water
- 1 tablespoon olive oil
- ½ small yellow onion, finely chopped
- ½ pound lean ground chuck
- 2 tablespoons tomato paste
- ½ teaspoon ground cumin
- ½ teaspoon dried oregano
- ¼ teaspoon salt
- ¼ teaspoon freshly ground black pepper
- 2 tablespoons chopped pimento-stuffed green olives
- 1 large egg, beaten with 1 teaspoon water, for egg wash

TO MAKE THE DOUGH

1. In the bowl of a food processor, pulse the flour, salt, and butter until the mixture looks like coarse crumbs. In a small bowl, whisk together the egg, water, and lemon juice. Add the egg mixture to the flour mixture, and process until the dough is evenly moistened and holds together when pressed between fingertips (add water by the tablespoon if needed). Form the dough into a disk, wrap it in plastic, and refrigerate for at least 30 minutes or up to overnight.

TO MAKE THE FILLING

2. In a bowl, soak the currants in the boiling water while you start the filling. In a large frying pan over medium heat, warm the olive oil. Add the onion and a pinch of salt, and cook, stirring, until tender and golden, about 5 minutes. Crumble the meat into the pan, and cook, stirring occasionally to break up the meat, until the meat is no longer pink, about 3 minutes. Pour off most of the fat from the pan. Return to medium heat, and add 3 tablespoons water, the tomato paste, cumin, oregano, salt, and pepper, and cook, stirring, until the mixture is thick, about 2 minutes. Remove from the heat. Drain the currants through a sieve, and add to the meat mixture along with the olives. Stir to combine. Season with more salt and pepper if needed. Let cool to room temperature, or transfer to an airtight container and refrigerate until ready to use, up to 3 days.

TO ASSEMBLE

3. Line two rimmed baking sheets with parchment paper. On a lightly floured work surface, roll out the dough into a ⅛-inch-thick round. Using a Christmas tree cookie cutter (or a cardboard stencil and a paring knife) that is approximately 4½ by 3½ inches, cut out as many shapes as you can, making sure there are an even number of each shape. (Alternatively, use a 4½-inch-round biscuit cutter.) Gather the dough scraps, roll them out, and cut out additional shapes (if the dough becomes too warm, refrigerate for about 15 minutes). You should have about 20 shapes. Transfer the shapes to a baking sheet, and refrigerate for 15 minutes.

4. Position two racks evenly in the middle of the oven, and preheat to 375°F. Lay half the shapes on a clean work surface. Brush them lightly with the egg wash. Place about 2 tablespoons of the filling in the center of each shape, leaving a ⅓-inch border. Top with the top piece, aligning the shapes. Press around the edges to enclose the filling, then use the tines of a fork to seal the empanadas. Transfer to the baking sheets, spacing them at least 1 inch apart. (The empanadas can be refrigerated at this point for up to 1 day.)

5. Brush the empanadas with the egg wash. Bake until golden brown, about 30 minutes. Remove from the oven and let cool for 5 minutes on the baking sheets on wire racks. Transfer the empanadas to a platter, and serve warm.

Man-Eating Wreath Burritos

Endlessly versatile, these yummy burritos will feed your most gruesome crowd. Serving them in the shape of the Man-Eating Wreath for guests to tear apart just adds to the festive fun. Personalize them with pickled onions, your favorite salsa, Mexican rice, guacamole, and sour cream. Make sure you adjust for the amounts with every additional ingredient.

Yield: 8 burritos | Difficulty: Medium

FOR THE CARNITAS

- 2½ to 3 pounds boneless pork shoulder, trimmed of large pieces of fat and reserved
- 1 teaspoon salt
- 1 cup fresh orange juice
- ¼ cup water
- 4 cloves garlic, peeled and crushed
- Avocado or canola oil, if needed

FOR THE BEANS

- 2 cups cooked pinto beans, rinsed and drained
- 3 tablespoons reserved carnitas cooking liquid
- Juice of ½ a small lime
- 3 tablespoons fresh cilantro, chopped and loosely packed

FOR THE BURRITOS

- Eight 10-inch spinach tortillas, warmed
- 1¾ cups Monterey Jack cheese, shredded
- 1 cup pico de gallo
- 2 sandwich-sized slices cheddar cheese
- 2 sandwich-sized slices Monterey Jack cheese
- 4 large cherry tomatoes
- 3 to 4 cups spinach leaves or shredded lettuce

TO MAKE THE CARNITAS

1. Preheat the oven to 300°F.

2. Cut the pork into three or four pieces. Add the pork to a Dutch oven just large enough to hold the pork in a single layer. Season all over with salt. Add the orange juice, water, and garlic. Bring to a boil over medium-high heat. Cover and transfer to the oven. Cook, turning the meat a few times, until the meat is very tender, about 3 hours. (Alternatively, use a slow cooker on the low heat setting for 8 hours.) Transfer the pork to a cutting board (reserve the cooking liquid). When it's cool enough to handle, using two forks, shred the pork, discarding any large pieces of fat or gristle. Transfer the pork to a bowl. Strain the cooking liquid through a fine-mesh sieve into a glass measuring pitcher; use a metal spoon to skim off the fat into another bowl.

TO MAKE THE BEANS

3. Add the cooked beans to a saucepan with the carnitas cooking liquid, lime juice, and the cilantro. Simmer over medium-low heat until warmed through, about 2 minutes. Cover to keep warm.

4. Add ¼ cup of the fat reserved from the pork shoulder into the Dutch oven, or use avocado oil or canola oil if preferred. Place over medium heat. When the fat is hot, add the carnitas. Cook, stirring occasionally and scraping up the browned bits, until the meat is crisped and browned, about 8 minutes. Add more fat if the meat seems dry. Stir in ¼ cup cooking liquid until warmed through. Cover to keep warm.

TO ASSEMBLE THE BURRITOS

5. Reduce the oven temperature to 200°F. Warm the tortillas on a baking sheet for a few minutes; remove the tortillas but leave the baking sheet in the oven. Lay the warm tortillas on a clean work surface. Top each with about ⅓ cup of carnitas and ¼ cup of beans in the bottom center of the tortilla, dividing evenly among the tortillas. Top with about 3 tablespoons cheese and 2 tablespoons pico de gallo. Fold the bottom of the tortilla over the filling, then fold the left and right sides of the tortilla over the filling. Tightly roll the bottom of the burrito to the top to complete the wrap. Place the burrito on the baking sheet, seam side down, to keep warm. The burritos can be covered with aluminum foil and kept warm in the oven for up to 30 minutes before serving.

TO MAKE THE MAN-EATING WREATH

6. Have a large serving board ready. Cut the cheddar cheese slices into two large evil eyes. Cut the Monterey Jack cheese slices into fangs. Arrange the burritos in a wreath shape, overlapping the burritos as needed to keep a tight shape. Place the evil eyes near the top of the wreath on the top two burritos. Add a halved cherry tomato, cut side down, onto each eye. Decorate the rest of the burritos with the remaining cherry tomatoes to look like ornaments. Arrange the cheese "teeth" on the board on the inside of the wreath. Arrange the spinach around the outer edge of the wreath. Serve at once.

Zero Barbecued Ribs

Meaty, thick barbecued spareribs can take hours of hands-on labor on the smoker, but this version makes use of the oven for most of the cooking to achieve tender ribs that Zero would love to fetch. A quick sear on a hot grill just before serving adds caramelization and flavor, but you can also easily finish them in the oven.

Yield: 6 to 8 servings | Difficulty: Medium

FOR THE RIBS

- 2 racks (about 6 pounds) pork spareribs
- 2 teaspoons salt
- 1 teaspoon smoked paprika
- 1 teaspoon dried oregano
- 1 teaspoon dried thyme
- 1 teaspoon granulated garlic
- 1 teaspoon onion powder
- 1 teaspoon freshly ground black pepper

FOR THE BARBECUE SAUCE

- ½ cup ketchup-style chili sauce
- ½ cup peach preserves
- 2 tablespoons unsulfured dark molasses
- 1 tablespoon apple cider vinegar
- 1 tablespoon Dijon mustard
- 1 teaspoon hot pepper sauce

- Avocado or canola oil

TO PREPARE THE RIBS

1. Preheat the oven to 350°F. Cut each rib rack into two or three sections. In a small bowl, mix together the salt, paprika, oregano, thyme, granulated garlic, onion powder, and pepper. Sprinkle the mixture on both sides of the ribs, and rub it into the meat.

2. Arrange the ribs, overlapping slightly, in a large roasting pan. Cover the pan tightly with aluminum foil, place in the oven, and roast for 45 minutes. Remove the foil, turn the ribs, and return to the oven uncovered. Continue cooking until the ribs are tender and browned, about 45 minutes more.

TO MAKE THE BARBECUE SAUCE

3. While the ribs cook, in a small saucepan over medium-low heat, stir together the chili sauce, peach preserves, molasses, vinegar, mustard, and hot pepper sauce. Bring to a gentle boil, then remove from the heat, and set aside.

4. Finish the ribs by preparing a grill for direct-heat cooking over medium-high heat. Brush the grill grate clean. Brush both sides of the ribs with the sauce. Place ribs on the grill, cover, and cook, turning once, until the ribs are nicely browned and glazed, about 10 minutes per side. (Alternatively, increase the oven temperature to 425°F. Pour off the fat in the roasting pan, then return the ribs to the pan. Brush the ribs with some of the sauce, and cook until the ribs are glazed, about 5 minutes. Turn, brush with more of the sauce, and cook to glaze the other side, about 5 minutes more.)

5. Transfer the ribs to a carving board. Let rest for 5 minutes. Cut between the bones into individual ribs, heap on a platter, and serve with any remaining sauce alongside.

Jack Skellington Cheese and Veggie Quesadillas

Adding a drizzle of hot sauce across these quesadillas gives them an extra splash of terror. The filling is endlessly versatile—you can omit the mushrooms and spinach for cheese quesadillas, or use just mushrooms or only spinach. Or spread refried beans on the underside of each tortilla and layer the cheese in the middle.

Yield: 4 quesadilla | Difficulty: Easy

- 1 tablespoon extra-virgin olive oil, plus more for brushing
- 2 cups cremini or button mushrooms, sliced
- Salt and freshly ground black pepper
- 3 cups baby spinach
- Eight 6-inch flour tortillas
- 1 cup shredded pepper Jack or Jack cheese
- Hot sauce, for serving (optional)

1. Place a rimmed baking sheet in the oven, and preheat to 200°F. In a frying pan, warm the olive oil over medium heat. Add the mushrooms, season with a little salt and pepper, and cook, stirring, until tender, about 4 minutes. Add the spinach, and cook until wilted, 1 to 2 minutes. Transfer to a bowl.

2. Place 4 tortillas on a work surface. For each tortilla, using a sharp paring knife, cut out two oval eyes, two small nostrils, and a wide grin, to look like Jack Skellington. Be careful to keep about 1 inch of the outside edge of the tortilla uncut. Brush each cut tortilla lightly with oil.

3. Brush the frying pan with a little oil. Place one uncut tortilla in the pan and spread 2 tablespoons shredded cheese over the tortilla, then top with ¼ of the spinach-mushroom mixture, spreading it into an even layer. Top with 2 tablespoons more shredded cheese, then top with one of the cutout tortillas. Make sure the cheese is tucked under the tortilla away from the eye cutouts. Cook over medium-low heat until golden on the bottom and the cheese starts to melt, about 2 minutes. Using a large spatula, carefully turn the quesadilla, then cook until the bottom is golden, about 1 minute longer. Gently transfer to the baking sheet in the oven, face side up, to keep warm while you finish the remaining quesadillas. Repeat to cook the other quesadillas. Serve hot, with hot sauce if you like.

TIP
Don't worry if any filling falls out—just tuck it back into the quesadilla before serving.

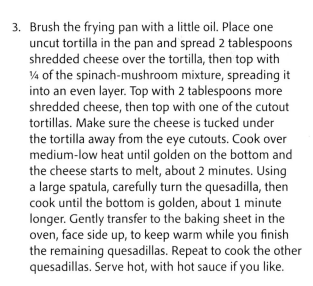

Desserts

Man-Eating Marshmallow Crispy Wreaths

Homemade Marshmallow Zero Dogs

Christmas Town Gingerbread Snowflakes With Spiders

The Mayor Two-Faced Black and White Cookies

Clown With a Tear-Away Face Lemon-Blackberry Macarons

Lock, Shock, and Barrel Spiral Peppermint Cookie Pops

Sandy Claws Iced Sugar Cookies

Christmas Town Cherry Lattice Pie

Jack Skellington Apple Hand Pies

Oogie Boogie Meringues

Jack Skellington White Chocolate Skull Bowls With Chocolate Mousse

White Chocolate Strawberry Ghosts

Snowy Grapefruit Granita

Mini Jack-O'-Lantern Cheesecakes

Oogie Boogie Lemon Meringue Cupcakes

Halloween Scaredy Canes

Oogie Boogie Double Chocolate Dirt Cake

Christmas Town Snowman Cupcakes

Sally Patchwork Layer Cake

Christmas Town is a dessert lover's dream. There are gingerbread-shaped houses and candy-cane-colored lampposts, ladders, and window sashes. Outside Santa's workshop are peppermint green mailboxes and lollipop window dressings. Even the snow that covers the village is its own version of frosting.

After Jack returns from his visit to Christmas Town, he contemplates the meaning of the holiday while bedded down in his tower at night. Nearby, his ghost dog, Zero, sleeps happily in his basket, a candy cane in his mouth. There's no sweeter way to end a day—or a meal—than with a confection that's sugary, crunchy, or creamy. And if it's all three, all the better. The desserts in this section are the perfect combination of the delectable sweets of Christmas Town and the devious essence of Halloween Town to create new and enchanting delights.

Man-Eating Marshmallow Crispy Wreaths

These Man-Eating Wreaths might look frightful, but they are so yummy they're hard to resist. When shaping the warm cereal mixture, be sure to work quickly and keep your hands well buttered to ensure the mixture doesn't stick. The royal icing does double duty here for both decorating and acting as glue to stick the marshmallow eyes and teeth onto the wreaths.

Yield: 15 wreaths | Difficulty: Medium

FOR THE MARSHMALLOW CRISPIES

- 3 tablespoons unsalted butter, plus more for hands
- One 10-ounce package mini marshmallows
- ⅛ teaspoon green gel food coloring, or more if needed
- 6 cups puffed rice cereal
- Cooking spray

FOR THE ROYAL ICING

- 1 ounce pasteurized egg whites, at room temperature
- ⅛ teaspoon cream of tartar
- Pinch of salt
- 1½ cups powdered sugar, sifted
- ⅛ teaspoon red gel food coloring, or more if needed

TO MAKE THE MARSHMALLOW CRISPIES

1. Line two large rimmed baking sheets with parchment paper. In a large saucepan over low heat, melt the butter. Add 4 cups (8 ounces) marshmallows, and cook, stirring, until completely melted. Stir in the green food coloring until well combined. Add the cereal, and stir until well coated. Remove from the heat, and let cool slightly.

2. Spray a ⅓ cup measuring cup lightly with cooking spray. Scoop up a portion of the cereal mixture, and transfer it to the prepared baking sheet. Using buttered hands, shape the mound into a small wreath. Working quickly, repeat with the remaining mixture, arranging the wreaths at least 1 inch apart and dividing between the two prepared baking sheets.

TO MAKE THE ROYAL ICING

3. In a bowl using an electric mixer with the whisk attachment, beat the egg whites, cream of tartar, and salt on medium-low speed until blended. With the machine running, add the sugar slowly. Increase the speed to medium-high, and beat until thick, stiff, and glossy, 7 to 8 minutes. Beat the red food coloring into the bowl of icing. (Cover with plastic wrap if not using immediately, up to 6 hours in advance.) Transfer the icing to a small piping bag fitted with a ⅛-inch round tip.

4. Use the remaining mini marshmallows for decorating. Cut fifteen mini marshmallows in half crosswise; these will be the eyes. Use the royal icing to pipe two dots for where the eyes will go and use it to "glue" on two marshmallow halves. Pipe a dot on each marshmallow and angry eyebrows above. Pipe a red bow at the bottom of each wreath.

5. For the teeth, cut mini marshmallows in quarters, "gluing" them on with the royal icing, about three teeth on the bottom and three teeth on top.

6. Set aside for the icing to harden, about 1 hour. Serve once set. The wreaths are best the day they are made. You can cover them with plastic wrap and store at room temperature for up to 2 days.

Homemade Marshmallow Zero Dogs

With a glowing orange nose and long flowing ears, Jack's ghost dog, Zero, is as adorable as he is loyal. These homemade marshmallow treats are shaped like Zero and are just as irresistible. You'll need a piping bag and a little patience, as the piping takes a bit of practice, but the results are well worth it!

Yield: About 16 dogs | Difficulty: Hard

- ⅓ cup cold water plus ¼ cup water
- 1 envelope (2½ teaspoons) unflavored gelatin
- ⅛ teaspoon cream of tartar
- Pinch of salt
- 1 cup granulated sugar, plus more for sprinkling

- 1 teaspoon light corn syrup
- ½ teaspoon vanilla extract
- ½ cup sparkle sugar
- 32 mini chocolate chips (about 1 tablespoon)
- About 16 orange candy-coated candies

1. In the bowl of a stand mixer fitted with the whisk attachment, add the ⅓ cup cold water. Sprinkle the gelatin over the water, then set aside for the gelatin to soften, about 5 minutes. Add the cream of tartar and salt. Set the mixer to medium-high speed, and beat until white and fluffy, about 2 minutes.

2. In a small saucepan over medium-high heat, combine the granulated sugar, ¼ cup water, and the corn syrup. Whisk gently until the sugar dissolves, then stop stirring. Cook, gently swirling the pan occasionally, until the mixture reaches 238°F on a candy thermometer (soft ball stage).

3. Set the mixer to medium-low speed, and carefully drizzle the hot sugar syrup into the gelatin mixture, aiming it between the beater and side of the bowl. Increase the speed to high, and whip the mixture until it is white and thick, about 5 minutes. Add the vanilla, and continue to beat until soft peaks form and the marshmallow mixture holds its shape, about 8 minutes longer.

4. Transfer about ¾ of the marshmallow mixture to a large pastry bag fitted with a ½-inch round tip. Transfer the remaining marshmallow mixture to a medium pastry bag fitted with a ¼-inch round tip. Use a plastic pastry scraper to scrape the sticky mixture down into the bag.

5. Line a large rimmed baking sheet with parchment paper, and spread the sparkle sugar on it in an even layer.

> "No, Zero. Down, boy. My, what a brilliant nose you have. The better to light my way!"
>
> —JACK SKELLINGTON

TIP

Sparkle sugar is a type of decorative sugar that features large crystals that have been polished to a shine and is more coarse than sanding sugar.

6. For each Zero ghost dog, using the larger bag with the larger tip, pipe a thick pear-shaped line that starts ¾ inch wide (this is the tail) and becomes 1½ inches wide (this is the front of the body); it should be about 2½ inches long. Continue piping a mound on top of the wider end that is the same width as the body and tapers into the head; it should be about 1½ inches tall. As you finish piping the head, release the pressure and pull up and away from the face to form a short snout. Using the smaller pastry bag, pipe two ears, releasing the pressure and pulling up and away to taper them. Push two mini chocolate chips into the face for eyes, and an orange candy into the snout for the nose. Working as quickly as possible, repeat with the remaining marshmallow mixture. Sprinkle each with sugar to lightly coat. Set aside until the marshmallows dry, about 2 hours.

7. Serve or store in a parchment-lined airtight container until ready to serve, or up to 1 week.

Christmas Town Gingerbread Snowflakes With Spiders

Jack discovers Christmas Town after opening the Christmas Door in the Hinterlands and being blown inside through a swirl of snowflakes to the snowy North Pole. Cut into the shapes of snowflakes, these spiced gingerbread cookies are decorated with royal icing, sparkling sugar, and ... a spider. You can even decorate some of the cookies as spiderwebs if you like, for a Christmas and Halloween mash-up.

Yield: About 20 cookies | Difficulty: Medium

- 2½ cups all-purpose flour
- 2 teaspoons ground ginger
- 1 teaspoon baking soda
- ½ teaspoon salt
- ½ teaspoon ground cinnamon
- ¼ teaspoon nutmeg
- 12 tablespoons (1½ sticks) unsalted butter, at room temperature
- ½ cup firmly packed light brown sugar
- ¼ cup granulated sugar
- 1 large egg
- ⅓ cup dark unsulfured molasses
- Royal Icing (page 64)
- A few drops black gel food coloring
- ¼ cup sparkle sugar, for decorating

1. In a medium bowl, whisk together the flour, ginger, baking soda, salt, cinnamon, and nutmeg. In the bowl of a stand mixer fitted with the beater attachment, beat the butter, brown sugar, and granulated sugar on medium-high speed until fluffy and lightened, about 1 minute. Add the egg, and beat until well combined; scrape down the side of the bowl with a rubber spatula. Add the molasses, and beat on low speed until combined. On low speed, add half the dry ingredients, mixing until blended, then add the remaining dry ingredients, mixing until blended. Scrape down the sides of the bowl, and mix again to make sure the dough is well combined. The dough will be soft. Press the dough into a ball, divide in half, then form each half into a disk. Wrap each disk in plastic. Refrigerate for at least 2 hours or up to 2 days.

2. Preheat the oven to 400°F. Line two large rimmed baking sheets with parchment.

3. Unwrap one dough disk and place on a lightly floured work surface. Roll out the dough into a ⅛-inch-thick round. Using a 4-inch snowflake-shaped cookie cutter, cut out as many shapes as you can. Transfer the cookie shapes to the prepared baking sheets, spacing them at least 1 inch apart. Press the dough scraps together, and roll out and cut as many shapes as you can. If the dough becomes too warm, wrap it in plastic and refrigerate for about 10 minutes. Once the baking sheets are full, refrigerate until ready to bake. Refrigerate the rest of the dough until the first batch is baked, then repeat.

4. Bake the cookies until lightly browned on the bottom, rotating the baking sheets between racks halfway through baking, about 7 minutes. Let stand on the baking sheets for 5 minutes, then transfer to wire racks to cool completely. Repeat to bake the remaining cookies.

5. Prepare the royal icing as directed; if the icing is too thick, thin it with a few drops of water until it is a smooth, pipeable consistency. Spoon 3 tablespoons of the icing into a small bowl, and stir in the black food coloring until well combined. Cover with plastic wrap. Transfer the remaining white icing to a small piping bag fitted with a small round tip ($\frac{1}{16}$ inch). For each snowflake, pipe crisscross lines from one side to the opposite. Pipe dots near where the lines intersect. At the ends of

each line, pipe Vs pointing toward the center to look like snowflake ends. Sprinkle with the sparkle sugar while the icing is wet. If you'd like, pipe half the cookies as snowflakes and the other half as spiderwebs. For each spiderweb, pipe crisscross lines from one side to the opposite. Create a web by connecting the ends of each line to the line next to it. Move slightly toward the center, and draw another series of lines between the lines. Repeat one more time. Replace the white icing with the black icing in the piping bag, and pipe spiders onto each cookie (or only the spiderwebs).

6. Leave the cookies on the wire rack until completely dry, at least 1 hour. Store in an airtight container, separated with parchment paper, for up to 3 days.

The Mayor Two-Faced Black and White Cookies

A naturally "two-faced" politician, the Mayor of Halloween Town reflects his mood by rotating his head from happy to dismayed. Based on the much-loved New York treat, these black and white cookies are tender and cake-like, with a shiny chocolate and vanilla glaze.

Yield: 12 large cookies | Difficulty: Easy

FOR THE COOKIES

- 1½ cups all-purpose flour
- ½ teaspoon baking powder
- ¼ teaspoon baking soda
- ¼ teaspoon salt
- 8 tablespoons (1 stick) unsalted butter, at room temperature
- ⅔ cup sugar
- 1 large egg, at room temperature
- 1 teaspoon vanilla extract
- ⅓ cup sour cream

FOR THE GLAZES

- 1½ cups powdered sugar
- 3 tablespoons milk, plus more as needed
- 1 tablespoon light corn syrup
- ½ teaspoon vanilla extract
- 3 tablespoons unsweetened Dutch-process cocoa powder

TO MAKE THE COOKIES

1. Preheat the oven to 350°F. Line a large rimmed baking sheet with parchment paper. In a small bowl, whisk together the flour, baking powder, baking soda, and salt. In the bowl of a stand mixer fitted with the paddle attachment, beat the butter and sugar on medium-high speed until lightened and creamy, about 1 minute. Scrape down the sides of the bowl with a rubber spatula, then beat in the egg and vanilla. With the mixer on low, add half the flour mixture, then the sour cream, then the other half of the flour mixture.

2. Using a ¼-cup scoop, scoop up the dough and arrange evenly on the prepared baking sheet; you should have twelve dough balls. Bake until puffed and cooked through with golden brown edges, about 15 minutes. Let the cookies cool on the baking sheet for about 5 minutes, then transfer to a wire rack to cool completely.

TO MAKE THE GLAZES

3. In a bowl, whisk together the powdered sugar, 2 tablespoons milk, corn syrup, and vanilla. Transfer ¼ cup of the glaze to another bowl, and whisk in the cocoa powder and remaining 1 tablespoon of milk. The glazes should be thick but easily spreadable; adjust the thickness by adding a little milk to thin the glaze, or more powdered sugar to thicken.

4. Turn the cookies upside down. On one half of each cookie, spread the vanilla icing on the flat bottom, leaving the other half free of icing. Refrigerate for 15 minutes or until set. Spread the chocolate icing onto the other half. Refrigerate for 15 minutes to set the icing. Serve. These cookies are best served the day they are made or within 1 day, but once the glaze is set, you can wrap them individually in plastic, and they will keep a few days longer.

Clown With a Tear-Away Face Lemon-Blackberry Macarons

These yellow and purple polka-dotted French-style macarons are dressed up just like the Clown with the Tear-Away Face but are probably more adorable than terrifying. Be sure to make them a day in advance so they have time to soften before you serve them.

Yield: 24 macarons | Difficulty: Hard

- 2 cups powdered sugar, divided
- 1⅓ cups superfine almond flour
- 3 large egg whites
- ½ teaspoon lemon extract
- ¼ teaspoon cream of tartar

- ⅛ teaspoon salt
- ⅛ teaspoon yellow gel food coloring
- A few drops purple gel food coloring
- About ¼ cup seedless blackberry jam

1. Using a 1½-inch-round biscuit cutter or glass, draw 24 circles on a sheet of parchment paper, spacing them 1 inch apart. Repeat with a second sheet of parchment. Turn the parchment paper over, and use each one to line a large rimmed baking sheet. Combine 1 cup of the powdered sugar and the almond flour in a sifter or fine-mesh sieve. Set aside.

2. In the bowl of a mixer fitted with the whisk attachment, beat the egg whites, lemon extract, cream of tartar, and salt on medium-high speed until foamy, about 30 seconds. Raise the speed to high, and gradually beat in the remaining 1 cup sugar, beating until stiff peaks form when the beaters are lifted (turn off the mixer first!), about 2 minutes longer.

3. Sift about one-third of the sugar-flour mixture over the beaten whites. Using a rubber spatula, gently fold it in just until blended. Repeat to fold in the remaining sugar-flour mixture in two more additions until incorporated. Fold the mixture until the ingredients are completely combined and the batter flows in a slow, thick ribbon (about 40 strokes). Transfer about 3 tablespoons of the batter to a small bowl. Add the yellow food coloring to the mixing bowl, and fold just until the color is uniform. Add the purple food coloring to the small bowl, and fold the mixture until the color is uniform.

4. Fit a large piping bag with a ⅜-inch round tip. Spoon the yellow batter into the piping bag. Fit a small piping bag with a 1/16-inch round tip. Spoon the purple batter into the piping bag. Gently twist the bags closed.

5. Holding the large piping bag with the tip about half an inch above the prepared cookie sheet, pipe mounds of yellow batter onto each sheet, using the circles as a guide. Pipe even mounds spaced about 1 inch apart, making the mounds as smooth as possible by moving the bag off to one side after piping each mound. Tap each sheet firmly against the work surface two or three times to release any air bubbles. Pipe purple polka dots on each of the yellow mounds of batter. Let the cookies stand at room temperature until they look less wet and are a little tacky, 45 to 60 minutes.

6. Preheat the oven to 300°F. Bake one sheet at a time until the cookies are risen and set but not browned, about 20 minutes. The bottoms of the cookies should be dry and firm to the touch and not stick to the parchment paper (if they stick, bake them a few minutes longer). Remove the cookie sheet from the oven, and set it on a wire rack. Let cool for 1 minute, then use a metal spatula to move the cookies directly to the rack. Repeat to bake the rest of the cookies. Let cool completely.

7. Spread about ½ teaspoon jam over the flat side of half the cookies. Top them with the remaining cookies, flat side down. Place the cookies in a single layer on a baking sheet, cover with plastic wrap, and refrigerate for at least 1 day or up to 3 days, or freeze for up to 6 months. Serve chilled or at cool room temperature (if frozen, thaw in the refrigerator before serving).

TIP

You can easily change the flavor profile of these cookies. Add vanilla extract in place of the lemon extract, and use your favorite frosting in the middle.

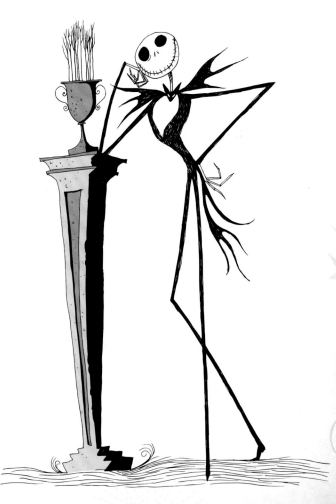

Lock, Shock, and Barrel Spiral Peppermint Cookie Pops

The trick-or-treating trio of Lock, Shock, and Barrel are the mischievous minions for Oogie Boogie who kidnap Santa after Jack orders them to. These cookies re-create the giant swirl of the lollipop Barrel likes to carry with him. If you like, leave out the peppermint and substitute vanilla or lemon extract.

Yield: 20 cookie pops | Difficulty: Medium

- 2 cups all-purpose flour
- 1 teaspoon baking powder
- ¼ teaspoon salt
- 12 tablespoons (1½ sticks) unsalted butter, at room temperature
- ¾ cup granulated sugar
- 1 large egg, separated

- 1 tablespoon milk
- ½ teaspoon peppermint extract or 1 teaspoon vanilla extract
- ⅛ teaspoon each red, black, and green gel food coloring, plus more if needed
- About ½ cup coarse decorating sugar, for rolling (optional)

1. In a medium bowl, whisk together the flour, baking powder, and salt. In the bowl of a mixer fitted with the paddle attachment, beat the butter and granulated sugar on medium speed until fluffy and pale, about 5 minutes. Turn off the mixer, and scrape down the bowl with a rubber spatula. Add the egg yolk and peppermint extract, and beat until combined. If too dry, add 1 tablespoon milk. Add half the flour mixture, and mix on low speed just until blended. Add the rest of the flour mixture, and mix just until the dough starts to clump together. Scrape down the bowl.

2. Turn the dough onto a clean work surface, and divide it into equal thirds. Add one third back to the bowl, and add the red food coloring, then gently knead until well combined and evenly colored. If your hands are slightly stained, wash your hands between colors to avoid transferring the color. Put one third of the dough into another bowl, and add the green food coloring, gently kneading it in until evenly colored. Put the remaining third of the dough into a bowl, and add the black food coloring, gently kneading it in until evenly colored. If the color is not as dark as you'd like, add more food coloring by gently kneading it into each third of the dough.

3. Have ready four sheets of parchment, each at least 15 by 12 inches. Set one dough third on the center of a sheet, and shape the dough into a rectangle. Cover with a second sheet, and roll out the dough into an 11-by-6½-inch rectangle. Remove the top sheet, slide the dough and parchment onto a baking sheet, and refrigerate. Repeat with the other two portions of dough.

4. In a small bowl, whisk together the egg white and 1 teaspoon water just until frothy. Remove and brush one dough rectangle lightly with the egg white, and place a second rectangle on top, lining up the edges. Repeat to brush the dough rectangle with egg white, and top with the third dough rectangle. Use a knife to even out the edges. Starting from a long side and using the parchment paper on the bottom piece of the dough to help, roll the dough into a log. If it starts to tear, gently pinch the dough back together. Roll the dough in the parchment to smooth it out.

5. If you'd like, scatter the coarse sugar on a rimmed cookie sheet, and roll the log in the sugar to coat the outside. Wrap the log tightly in plastic, and refrigerate until firm, at least 1 hour or up to overnight.

6. Position two racks evenly in the oven, and preheat to 350°F. Line two baking sheets with parchment paper. Unwrap the dough log, and set it on a cutting board. Trim off the ends, then cut the log crosswise into ½-inch-thick slices. Place the slices on the prepared baking sheet and chill for about 10 minutes. Remove from the refrigerator and insert a wooden ice-pop stick or a treat stick into the side of each cookie spiral. Place the slices on the prepared baking sheets, spacing them about 2 inches apart.

7. Bake, rotating the pans to opposite racks halfway through baking, until the cookies are firm to the touch and only starting to brown around the edges, 14 to 17 minutes. Let cool on the pans for 5 minutes, then transfer to a wire rack. Repeat to bake any remaining cookies in the same way. Let the cookies cool completely, and serve.

Sandy Claws Iced Sugar Cookies

Jack might try to send Sandy Claws on vacation and replace traditional Christmas with his own slightly terrifying version, but there is no substitute for the real Santa, who fixes Christmas in the end. These classic sugar cookies are a tribute to the ruler of the holiday world Christmas Town. Keep a portion of the royal icing thick enough to pipe outlines, and then thin the remaining to "flood" the cookies with a smooth layer of icing.

Yield: About 16 cookies | Difficulty: Hard

FOR THE SUGAR COOKIES

- 2 cups all-purpose flour
- ½ teaspoon baking powder
- ¼ teaspoon salt
- 8 tablespoons (1 stick) unsalted butter, at room temperature
- ¾ cup sugar
- 1 large egg
- 1½ teaspoons vanilla extract

FOR THE ROYAL ICING

- Royal icing (page 64)
- ¼ teaspoon red gel food coloring
- 32 mini chocolate chips

TO MAKE THE COOKIES

1. In a bowl, whisk together the flour, baking powder, and salt. In the bowl of a mixer fitted with the paddle attachment, beat the butter and sugar on medium speed until well blended, about 1 minute. Beat in the egg and vanilla until combined. Mix in the flour mixture on low speed just until the dough starts to clump together. Divide the dough in half, and press each half into a thick disk. Wrap in plastic. Refrigerate for at least 1 hour or up to overnight.

2. Position two racks evenly in the middle of the oven, and preheat to 350°F. Line two large rimmed baking sheets with parchment paper.

3. Unwrap one dough disk, and place on a lightly floured work surface. Roll out the dough into a ¼-inch-thick round. Using a 3- or 4-inch Santa-shaped cookie cutter, cut out as many shapes as you can. Transfer the cookie shapes to the prepared baking sheets. Press the dough scraps together, and roll out and cut as many shapes as you can. If the dough becomes too warm, wrap it in plastic and refrigerate for about 10 minutes. Repeat with the second dough disk, until all the dough is used. Refrigerate the cookies on the baking sheets until ready to bake.

4. Bake the cookies until lightly golden brown, rotating the baking sheets between racks halfway through baking, 10 to 14 minutes. Let cool on the pan on a wire rack for 5 minutes, then transfer the cookies to the rack to cool.

TO MAKE THE ROYAL ICING

5. Prepare the royal icing as directed; if the icing is too thick, thin it with a few drops of water until it is a smooth, pipeable consistency

6. Put one third of the icing in a separate bowl, and add the red food coloring; beat until well combined. Cover with plastic wrap. Leave the remaining icing white. Transfer half the white icing to a small piping bag fitted with a small round tip (1⁄16 inch). Use this to outline Santa's beard and the fluffy white parts of his hat. Pipe two dots for eyes, and top each dot with a mini chocolate chip.

7. Thin the remaining white icing to flood consistency, adding a few drops of water at a time. Clean out the piping bag, and add the flooding icing. Flood the beard and fluffy white parts of Santa's hat. Clean out the piping bag, and add half the red icing. Use this to outline Santa's hat and pipe a nose and smile on each Santa. Thin the remaining red icing to flood consistency, adding a few drops of water at a time. Clean out the piping bag, and add the flooding icing. Use this to flood Santa's hat.

8. Leave the cookies on the wire rack until completely dry, at least 1 hour. Store in an airtight container, separated with parchment, for up to 3 days.

Christmas Town Cherry Lattice Pie

When Jack discovers Christmas Town, he is enamored with all the new sights and sounds, where the "smells of cakes and pies are absolutely everywhere." This latticed cherry pie is pretty enough for a holiday bakeshop window.

Yield: 8 servings | Difficulty: Hard

FOR THE FLAKY PIE DOUGH (DOUBLE CRUST)

- 2½ cups all-purpose flour
- 1 tablespoon sugar
- ½ teaspoon salt
- 1 cup (2 sticks) very cold unsalted butter, cut into cubes
- ⅔ cup ice-cold water, plus more if needed

FOR THE CHERRY PIE FILLING

- 1 cup sugar
- 2 tablespoons tapioca starch
- ¼ teaspoon salt
- 4 cups jarred or canned pitted sour cherries, drained (reserve ⅓ cup cherry liquid)
- 1 teaspoon vanilla extract
- 1 tablespoon cold unsalted butter, cut into small pieces
- 1 egg, beaten with 1 teaspoon water, for egg wash
- 2 tablespoons sparkle sugar, for garnish

TO MAKE THE PIE DOUGH

1. In the bowl of a food processor, pulse together the flour, sugar, and salt. Sprinkle the butter over the top, and pulse until the butter is in pieces the size of small peas. Evenly sprinkle the water over the flour mixture, then process until the mixture starts to come together. Turn the dough onto a work surface, press it together, then divide it in half. Press each half into a disk, then wrap each disk in plastic. Refrigerate the dough for 30 minutes or up to 1 day, or freeze for up to 1 month.

2. Unwrap the dough disks, and transfer them to a lightly floured work surface. Roll each half into a round at least 12 inches in diameter and about ⅛ inch thick. Transfer one round to a 9-inch pie pan and ease into the pan. Trim the edge, leaving a 1-inch overhang. Refrigerate the dough-lined pan and dough round until ready to use.

TO MAKE THE FILLING

3. Preheat the oven to 375°F. In a small bowl, stir together the sugar, tapioca starch, and salt. Place the cherries in a large bowl, sprinkle with the sugar mixture, and toss to distribute evenly. Add the vanilla and the cherry liquid, and mix well. Pour the cherry mixture into the dough-lined pan, and dot with the butter.

4. Lay the second dough round on a lightly floured work surface, and using a 1-inch-wide ruler as a guide, cut nine to ten strips of dough. Arrange the dough strips in a lattice on top of the filling: Lay half of the strips on top of the pie, spacing them evenly apart. Fold back every other strip halfway and lay down a strip perpendicular across the unfolded strips, then unfold the strips back in place. Fold back the alternate strips, and repeat to lay down a strip perpendicular. Repeat to place the remaining strips of dough evenly across the top, folding back the alternate strips each time. Trim the edges, leaving a 1-inch overhang around the edge of the pie dish.

5. Tuck the dough under itself to create a rim that sits on top of the edge of the pie dish. Use your fingers or a fork to create a decorative rim. Brush the crust with the egg mixture. Sprinkle the top all over with the sparkle sugar. Place the pie dish on a baking sheet.

6. Bake until the crust is golden and the filling is thick and bubbling, about 1 hour. If the crust is starting to brown too quickly, cover it loosely with foil to avoid burning. Remove from oven and let cool completely on a wire rack to set the filling, then serve.

Jack Skellington Apple Hand Pies

Jack Skellington longs to find something to make Halloween more interesting, and when he stumbles upon Christmas, he thinks he has solved his problems. But instead of making things better, he turns Christmas macabre. With their wide skeleton grins and eerie cutout eyes, these Jack-inspired individual apple pies may solve all your dessert problems.

Yield: 10 mini pies | Difficulty: Medium

- Flaky Pie Dough, double crust (page 78)
- 2 tablespoons unsalted butter
- 1½ pounds tart-sweet baking apples, such as Gala, Pink Lady, or Honeycrisp, peeled, cored, and cut into ⅛-inch slices
- ¼ cup firmly packed light brown sugar
- 2 teaspoons fresh lemon juice
- ¼ teaspoon ground cinnamon
- ⅛ teaspoon salt
- 1 large egg, beaten with 1 teaspoon water, for egg wash

1. Make the pie dough, and refrigerate for 30 minutes as directed. In a large frying pan over medium heat, melt the butter. Add the apples, sugar, lemon juice, cinnamon, and salt. Cook, stirring occasionally, until the apples are just tender, about 7 minutes. Remove from the heat, and let cool to room temperature.

2. Line two large rimmed baking sheets with parchment paper. On a lightly floured work surface, roll out the pie dough into a large ⅛-inch-thick round. Using a 4-inch round cutter, cut out twenty rounds, gathering the scraps of dough and rerolling once. Transfer the rounds to one of the baking sheets, and cover with a piece of parchment. Refrigerate for 15 minutes.

3. Arrange five of the dough rounds on each baking sheet, spacing them apart. Brush lightly with egg wash, then mound ¼ cup of the apple filling in the center of each, leaving a ½-inch border. Lay the remaining dough rounds on a work surface, and using a ¾- to 1-inch round cutter (or a paring knife), cut out two eyes toward the center of each round. Lay a dough round over the top of the apple-topped rounds on the baking sheets. Gently press the dough round down over the filling, adhering it to the bottom round. Crimp the edges with the tines of a fork. Refrigerate for 15 minutes.

4. While the pies chill, position two racks evenly in the oven, and preheat to 400°F.

5. Brush the top of each hand pie lightly with the egg wash. Using a paring knife, cut a wide smiling mouth just above the crimped edge and follow the contour of the hand pie. Add a few crosscuts to look like Jack Skellington's grin. Be careful not to cut all the way through the pastry. Bake, rotating the pans to different racks halfway through, until the crust is golden brown and the filling is bubbling, about 25 minutes. Let cool on the pans set on wire racks for at least 15 minutes before serving.

Oogie Boogie Meringues

Big flat blobs of meringue tinted green are an ominous reminder of Oogie Boogie, but you won't find bugs, worms, and spiders inside these treats. These don't take a lot of hands-on time, but they do need to cook in a low oven and then cool there for a few hours in order to achieve their crispy-chewy texture.

Yield: About 24 meringues | Difficulty: Easy

- 4 large egg whites
- ⅛ teaspoon salt
- 1 cup sugar
- 1 teaspoon cornstarch

- 2 teaspoons vanilla extract
- ½ teaspoon white vinegar
- ⅛ teaspoon green gel food coloring, or as needed
- 48 mini chocolate chips

1. Preheat the oven to 325°F. Line a large rimmed baking sheet with parchment paper. Have ready a pastry bag fitted with a ½-inch plain tip.

2. In the bowl of a stand mixer fitted with the whisk attachment, beat the egg whites and salt on medium speed until foamy. With the mixer on, slowly add the sugar, beating until the egg whites are thick and glossy and the meringue holds a mostly stiff peak when the whisk attachment is turned upside down. Sift the cornstarch over the mixture, then add the vanilla, vinegar, and food coloring. Beat just until well combined.

3. Using a rubber spatula, scoop the meringue into the prepared pastry bag. Holding the bag straight up and down over the baking sheet, pipe fat mounds of meringue, each about 2 inches tall with a fat base and a smaller top with a curled end. Press two mini chocolate chips into each meringue for eyes.

4. Bake for 10 minutes, then reduce the oven temperature to 250°F. Bake until crisp, about 1 hour longer. Turn off the oven, and leave the meringues in the oven to cool completely, at least 2 hours or up to overnight. Serve at once, or store in an airtight container at room temperature for up to 1 week.

Jack Skellington White Chocolate Skull Bowls With Chocolate Mousse

Always dapper in his pin-striped suit, Jack Skellington is the Halloween version of elegance. These elegant desserts deserve a place at your next dinner party or even a romantic dinner for two. Serve on their own or with sliced strawberries or fresh raspberries.

Yield: 6 servings | Difficulty: Hard

FOR THE WHITE CHOCOLATE SKULL BOWLS
- 1 cup white chocolate chips
- 1 tablespoon vegetable shortening
- 6 small balloons
- 2 ounces bittersweet chocolate, finely chopped

FOR THE CHOCOLATE MOUSSE
- 10 ounces bittersweet chocolate, finely chopped
- 1½ cups heavy cream
- ½ cup powdered sugar
- 1 teaspoon vanilla extract

FOR SERVING
- Lightly whipped cream, for serving (optional)
- 6 strawberries, sliced (optional)

TO MAKE THE BOWLS

1. Line a rimmed baking sheet with parchment paper or waxed paper and place it in the refrigerator to chill. In a microwave-safe bowl, combine the white chocolate chips and shortening. Microwave on high, stirring every 20 seconds, just until the mixture is melted and smooth. Let the mixture cool until barely warm, about 10 minutes. Meanwhile, blow up six small balloons, and knot each one at the end. If you'd like, grease the lower half of the balloon with a bit of additional vegetable shortening to make it easier to release the balloons later.

2. Remove the baking tray from the refrigerator. When the chocolate has cooled, hold a balloon by the knotted end and dip it into the melted chocolate, covering 2½ to 3 inches of the balloon bottom. Place the chocolate-dipped balloon, chocolate side down, on the prepared baking sheet. You may need to hold the balloon steady for a few moments to make sure the balloon stays upright. Dip the remaining balloons and place on the baking sheet, then transfer to the refrigerator until the chocolate is set, about 10 minutes.

3. To decorate the white chocolate bowls, melt the 2 ounces chocolate in a microwave-safe bowl, stirring every 20 seconds, until smooth. Let cool. Transfer the cooled chocolate to a small piping bag fitted with a ⅛-inch round tip. Hold the balloon knot as you draw oval eyes and a mouth like Jack Skellington's face on the side of each cup.

4. Pop the balloons with a pin and gently remove the balloon bits from the bowls. Return the bowls to the refrigerator until ready to serve, up to 1 day in advance.

TO MAKE THE MOUSSE

5. Bring 1 inch of water in a small saucepan to a simmer over medium-low heat. Put the chopped chocolate and ½ cup of the heavy cream in a heatproof bowl that is slightly larger than the saucepan and place it on the saucepan, making sure that the bowl does not touch the simmering water below. Heat, stirring often, until melted and smooth, about 5 minutes. Let cool completely. (To speed cooling, nestle the bowl of chocolate in a large bowl filled with ice-cold water, and stir until the chocolate is room temperature.)

6. In a bowl, combine the remaining heavy cream, powdered sugar, and vanilla. Beat with an electric mixer on medium-high speed until firm peaks form. Scoop about one-third of the whipped cream on top of the cooled chocolate and whisk gently until blended and smooth. Using a rubber spatula, gently fold the remaining whipped cream into the chocolate mixture just until combined. Do not overwork, or you will deflate the mousse.

7. Spoon the mousse into the white chocolate cups. Cover and refrigerate for at least 2 hours or up to overnight. If desired, spoon a small dollop of whipped cream and a sprinkling of fresh strawberries into each cup before serving.

White Chocolate Strawberry Ghosts

Flying through the eerie graveyard into Halloween Town, spectral spirits sing about Halloween. These chocolate-dipped strawberries use white chocolate instead of dark to mimic ghosts. .

Yield: 12 strawberries | Difficulty: Easy

- 1 cup white chocolate chips
- 1 tablespoon vegetable shortening
- 12 large fresh strawberries, rinsed and dried
- ¼ cup semisweet chocolate chips

1. Line a baking sheet with parchment paper. Place the white chocolate chips and shortening in a heatproof bowl set over (not touching) barely simmering water, and heat, stirring occasionally with a rubber spatula, just until melted and smooth, about 5 minutes. Remove from the heat.

2. Holding each strawberry by its green hull or stem, dip it into the melted chocolate until it is about three-quarters covered. Use the spatula, if necessary, to help coat each strawberry with chocolate. Let the excess chocolate drip back into the bowl, then place each strawberry on the baking sheet.

3. Refrigerate the coated strawberries on the baking sheet until the chocolate sets, about 15 minutes. When the white chocolate is set, in a microwavable bowl, melt the semisweet chocolate chips in the microwave in 20-second bursts, stirring after every 20 seconds, until melted and smooth.

4. Using a toothpick or a wooden skewer, draw eyes and a ghoulish mouth on each strawberry. Return the strawberries to the baking sheet, and let set.

5. The strawberries are best eaten within a day. If necessary, cover loosely with parchment paper, and store overnight in the refrigerator. Bring to room temperature before serving.

TIP

If the white chocolate starts to firm up before you are finished dipping the strawberries, put it in the microwave, stirring about every 10 seconds, until melted.

Snowy Grapefruit Granita

The sparkling snow and twinkling lights of Christmas Town are unlike anything Jack has ever seen. This glittering granita, a semi-frozen Italian dessert, sparkles with fresh grapefruit flavor. Stirring regularly while the mixture freezes is what gives the ice crystals their fine texture.

Yield: 4 to 6 servings | Difficulty: Easy

- ¾ cup sugar
- ¾ cup water
- 2 teaspoons grated grapefruit zest
- 1½ cups unsweetened grapefruit juice

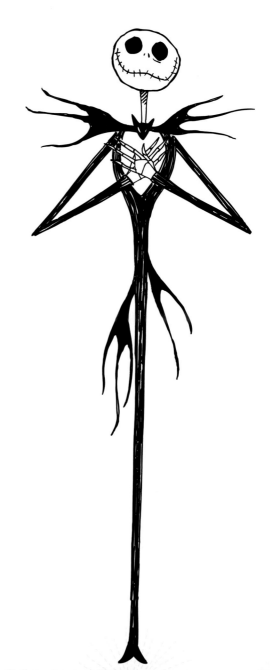

1. In a small saucepan, stir together the sugar, water, and grapefruit zest. Place over medium-high heat, and bring to a steady boil. Boil, stirring frequently, until the syrup is clear with no visible grains of sugar, 1 to 2 minutes. Remove from the heat, pour into a bowl, and let cool to room temperature, about 20 minutes. Cover the bowl with plastic wrap, and refrigerate until the syrup is very cold, about 1 hour.

2. Pour the chilled grapefruit syrup through a fine-mesh sieve set over a bowl, pressing on the zest with the back of a spoon. Stir the grapefruit juice into the syrup. Pour the mixture into a shallow metal baking pan. Freeze, stirring with a whisk every 30 minutes, until the mixture is semi-firm, about 3 hours. Cover with plastic wrap, and return to the freezer without stirring until frozen solid, at least 8 hours or up to 24 hours.

3. At least 1 hour before serving, place four to six glasses in the freezer. To serve, using a fork, scrape the surface of the granita into fine ice crystals. Scoop the granita "snowballs" into the frozen glasses. Serve right away.

Mini Jack-O'-Lantern Cheesecakes

Jack-o'-lanterns adorn the spiky fence surrounding the Halloween Town graveyard. Make your own patch of jack-o'-lanterns with these individual spiced pumpkin cheesecakes. Take them to the next level by piping a grinning (or terrifying) jack-o'-lantern face on each dessert. And then watch them disappear like the night.

Yield: 16 mini cheesecakes | Difficulty: Easy

FOR THE GINGERSNAP CRUST
- ¾ cup gingersnap cookie crumbs
- 3 tablespoons unsalted butter, melted and cooled
- 1 tablespoon firmly packed light brown sugar

FOR THE PUMPKIN FILLING
- Two 8-ounce packages cream cheese, at room temperature
- ⅔ cup firmly packed light brown sugar

- ⅔ cup canned pumpkin purée
- 1 teaspoon vanilla extract
- ½ teaspoon pumpkin pie spice
- 2 large eggs
- 1 tablespoon all-purpose flour
- ⅓ cup semisweet chocolate chips (optional)

TO MAKE THE CRUST

1. Preheat the oven to 325°F. Line 16 cups of two 12-cup standard muffin pans.

2. In a bowl, stir together the gingersnap crumbs, melted butter, and brown sugar until well combined and the crumbs stick together. Divide the mixture evenly among the prepared muffin cups (1 tablespoon per cup). Press the crumbs into the bottom of each cup with the bottom of a small glass. Bake until set, about 5 minutes. Remove the pans from the oven, and set them on wire racks to cool slightly.

TO MAKE THE FILLING

3. In the bowl of a food processor, process the cream cheese and brown sugar on medium speed until smooth, about 2 minutes. Scrape down the sides of the bowl with a rubber spatula. Add the pumpkin purée, vanilla, and pumpkin pie spice, and process until blended. Add the eggs one at a time, processing after each addition. Add the flour, and process until combined. Scrape down the bowl, and process once more.

4. Divide the filling evenly among the prepared muffin cups, filling each nearly full. Bake until the cheesecakes are set but still a little jiggly in the center, 18 to 20 minutes. Remove the pans from the oven, and set them on wire racks to cool completely.

5. If you want to decorate the cheesecakes, melt the chocolate chips in a microwave-safe bowl in 20-second bursts on high, stirring after every 20 seconds. Transfer the melted chocolate to a small pastry bag with a very small round tip, and draw a jack-o'-lantern face on the top of each cheesecake. (Alternatively, use a toothpick to draw the faces.)

6. Cover with plastic wrap, and refrigerate until chilled, at least 3 hours or up to overnight. Serve.

Oogie Boogie Lemon Meringue Cupcakes

Sinister and power-hungry Oogie Boogie loves gambling and theatrics. Green-tinted, lemon-scented cupcakes topped with a gooey marshmallow meringue frosting may resemble Oogie Boogie, but there's nothing to be afraid of—they taste (and smell) incredible!

Yield: 18 cupcakes | Difficulty: Medium

FOR THE LEMON CUPCAKES

- 2 cups all-purpose flour
- 2 teaspoons baking powder
- ½ teaspoon baking soda
- ½ teaspoon salt
- 10 tablespoons (1¼ sticks) unsalted butter, at room temperature
- ¾ cup sugar
- Finely grated zest of 1 large lemon
- 2 large eggs
- ⅛ teaspoon green gel food coloring
- 1¼ cups buttermilk
- 2 tablespoons fresh lemon juice

FOR THE MERINGUE FROSTING

- 2 large egg whites, at room temperature
- ⅔ cup sugar
- 1 tablespoon light corn syrup
- ⅛ teaspoon salt
- ¼ cup water
- 1 teaspoon vanilla extract
- ⅛ teaspoon green gel food coloring

TO MAKE THE CUPCAKES

1. Preheat the oven to 375°F. Line 18 cups of two 12-cup standard muffin pans.

2. In a small bowl, whisk together the flour, baking powder, baking soda, and salt. In the bowl of a stand mixer fitted with the beater attachment, beat the butter, sugar, and lemon zest on medium-high speed until light and fluffy, about 2 minutes. Add the eggs one at a time, beating well after each addition. Scrape down the sides of the bowl with a rubber spatula. Add the green food coloring and a third of the flour mixture and mix on low speed just until blended. Add half the buttermilk and the lemon juice and mix on low speed until combined. Add another third of the flour mixture, then the remaining buttermilk and mix just until

blended. Add the remaining flour mixture and beat until blended. Scrape down the sides of the bowl and give the batter a stir. Divide the batter evenly among the prepared muffin cups, filling them about three-quarters full.

3. Bake until the tops are puffed and a toothpick inserted into the center of a cupcake comes out clean, about 20 minutes. Remove the pans from the oven and set them on a wire rack. Let cool for 10 minutes, then carefully transfer the cupcakes directly to the rack. Let cool completely, about 1 hour.

TO MAKE THE MERINGUE FROSTING

4. In a heatproof bowl, whisk together the egg whites, sugar, corn syrup, salt, and water. Set the bowl over (but not touching) barely simmering water in a saucepan. Using an electric hand mixer fitted with the whisk attachment, beat on medium-high speed to stiff peaks, about 5 minutes. Remove the bowl from over the water and continue to beat until the mixture cools, about 2 minutes. Add the vanilla and food coloring and beat until blended.

5. Transfer the frosting to a large piping bag fitted with a ½-inch round tip. Holding the piping bag perpendicular to the cupcake, pipe an Oogie Boogie blob of frosting onto each cupcake. Add two mini chocolate chips for eyes. Serve at once, or refrigerate for up to 1 day before serving. These are best served the day they are made.

Halloween Scaredy Canes

Candy canes decorate much of Christmas Town, but these twisted chocolate-orange cookies turn the Christmas classic into a Halloween treat. Sugar cookie dough is divided, then flavored with orange zest and cocoa.

Yield: 14 cookies | Difficulty: Medium

- 1¾ cups all-purpose flour, divided
- ½ teaspoon baking powder
- ¼ teaspoon salt
- 8 tablespoons (1 stick) unsalted butter, at room temperature
- ¾ cup sugar

- 1 large egg
- 1 teaspoon vanilla extract
- 1 teaspoon finely grated orange zest
- ⅛ teaspoon orange gel food coloring
- 3 tablespoons cocoa powder

1. In a bowl, whisk together 1½ cups flour, baking powder, and salt. In the bowl of a mixer fitted with the paddle attachment, beat the butter and sugar on medium speed until well blended, about 1 minute. Beat in the egg and vanilla until combined. Gradually beat in the flour mixture on low speed just until blended. Scrape down the bowl with a rubber spatula. Divide the dough in half; the dough will be soft. Leave one half in the mixing bowl, and transfer the other half to the bowl that had the flour in it.

2. Add the remaining ¼ cup flour, orange zest, and orange food coloring to the dough in the mixing bowl. Mix on low speed until fully combined. Form the dough into a disk, and wrap in plastic. Wipe out the mixing bowl, and add the other half of the dough. Sift the cocoa powder over the dough, then mix on low speed until fully combined. Form the dough into a disk, and wrap in plastic. Refrigerate both dough disks for at least 1 hour or up to overnight.

3. Position two racks evenly in the oven, and preheat to 350°F. Line two baking sheets with parchment paper. Let the dough soften slightly before rolling, about 15 minutes.

4. On a lightly floured work surface, roll out each dough disk into a rectangle about 6 by 11 inches and ¼ inch thick. Place the dough rectangles side by side on one of the prepared baking sheets. Refrigerate for 15 minutes.

5. Transfer the dough back to the cutting board, and cut each rectangle crosswise into strips 6 inches long and ½ inch wide. For each cookie, gently roll one chocolate strip and one orange strip into a rough rope about 7 inches long. If the orange dough is too soft, it's okay to leave each strip chilling in the refrigerator until you twist together. Pinch the ends of the two ropes together, and gently twist the strips around each other. Pinch the other end to secure, and bend one end into a hook to form a candy cane shape. Transfer to the baking sheet. Repeat with the remaining dough, spacing the cookies about 1½ inches apart. (If the dough gets too soft and tears a lot, refrigerate it for about 10 minutes before continuing.)

6. Bake, rotating the pans between the racks halfway through, until the cookies are golden on the edges, about 13 minutes. Let cool completely on the baking sheets set on wire racks. Serve or store in an airtight container for up to 1 week.

Oogie Boogie Double Chocolate Dirt Cake

After trying his best to get rid of Santa, Sally, and Jack, Oogie Boogie gets his own undoing when Jack unravels his burlap sack and a shower of bugs falls into the lava pit below. This rich coffee and dark chocolate cake topped with creamy frosting and cookie "dirt" is a great place to capture gummy worms and bugs.

Yield: 12 servings | Difficulty: Easy

FOR THE CHOCOLATE MOCHA CAKE

- Cooking spray
- 2 cups all-purpose flour
- 2 teaspoons baking powder
- 1 teaspoon baking soda
- 1 cup brewed strong coffee
- 6 ounces dark chocolate, chopped
- ⅔ cup natural cocoa powder
- 1 cup buttermilk
- 8 tablespoons (1 stick) unsalted butter, at cool room temperature
- 1½ cups firmly packed light brown sugar
- ¼ cup avocado or canola oil
- 1 teaspoon salt
- 3 large eggs
- 2 teaspoons vanilla extract

FOR THE CHOCOLATE FROSTING

- 2 cups powdered sugar
- ½ cup natural cocoa powder
- 6 tablespoons (¾ stick) unsalted butter, at cool room temperature
- ⅓ cup whole milk
- 1 teaspoon vanilla extract
- Pinch of salt

FOR THE TOPPINGS

- 1½ cups chocolate wafer cookie crumbs
- 12 gummy worms

TO MAKE THE CAKE

1. Preheat the oven to 350°F. Spray a 9-by-13-inch baking dish with cooking spray. In a bowl, whisk together the flour, baking powder, and baking soda. Set aside.

2. In a saucepan over medium-low heat, warm the coffee. Add the chocolate, and whisk gently until melted and smooth. Remove from the heat, sift the cocoa powder over the coffee mixture, and whisk to combine. Add the buttermilk, and whisk to combine. Set aside to cool to room temperature.

3. In the bowl of a stand mixer fitted with the beater attachment, beat the butter, brown sugar, oil, and salt on medium speed until creamy, about 1 minute. Add the eggs one at a time, beating after each addition. Scrape down the sides of the bowl with a rubber spatula. Beat in the vanilla, then add the chocolate mixture, and beat until combined. Add the flour mixture, and mix on low speed just until incorporated. Scrape down the sides of the bowl then mix again just until well combined. Pour the batter into the prepared baking dish, and smooth the top.

4. Bake the cake until a wooden skewer inserted into the center of the cake comes out clean, about 45 minutes. Transfer to a wire rack, and let the cake cool completely.

TO MAKE THE FROSTING

5. Into the clean bowl of the stand mixer, sift together the powdered sugar and cocoa. Add the butter, and mix on low speed until the mixture is crumbly. Beat in the milk, vanilla, and salt on medium-high speed until smooth and fluffy. Scrape down the sides of the bowl, and mix again.

6. Spread the frosting over the top and sides of the cooled cake. Sprinkle the cookie crumbs over the top of the cake in an even layer. Decorate with the gummy worms. Serve at once, or refrigerate for up to 4 days.

Christmas Town Snowman Cupcakes

When Jack arrives in Christmas Town he uses a snowman to disguise himself from the local residents while he tries to understand what Christmas is all about. Fluffy white cream cheese frosting disguises the tender red velvet cupcakes underneath, and candies create a snowman's face.

Yield: 16 to 18 cupcakes | Difficulty: Easy

FOR THE RED VELVET CUPCAKES

- 2 cups all-purpose flour
- 1 teaspoon baking soda
- ¼ teaspoon salt
- 2 tablespoons unsweetened cocoa powder, sifted
- ¼ cup boiling water
- 1 cup buttermilk
- 12 tablespoons (1½ sticks) unsalted butter, at room temperature
- 1 cup sugar
- 2 large eggs
- 2 teaspoons vanilla extract
- 1 teaspoon white vinegar
- ⅛ teaspoon red gel food coloring, or as needed

FOR THE CREAM CHEESE FROSTING

- 12 ounces cream cheese, at room temperature
- 6 tablespoons (¾ stick) unsalted butter, at room temperature
- 2 teaspoons vanilla extract
- 1½ cups powdered sugar, sifted

- About ¼ cup chocolate chips
- 16 to 18 candy corns
- About ¼ cup mini chocolate chips
- About 4 green sour candy strips

TO MAKE THE CUPCAKES

1. Preheat the oven to 350°F. Line 16 to 18 cups of two 12-cup standard muffin pans. In a bowl, whisk together the flour, baking soda, and salt. In a heatproof bowl, whisk together the cocoa and the boiling water, then whisk in the buttermilk. In the bowl of a mixer fitted with the beater attachment, beat the butter and sugar on medium-high speed until fluffy and pale, about 3 minutes. Add the eggs one at a time, beating well after adding each one. Add the vanilla, vinegar, and food coloring, and beat until combined. Turn off the mixer, and scrape down the bowl with a rubber spatula. Add half the flour mixture, then the buttermilk mixture, and finally the remaining flour mixture, beating on low speed just until blended. Scrape down the sides of the bowl, then adjust the amount of food coloring as desired. Mix on low speed for 10 more seconds.

2. Using a quarter-cup scoop, divide the batter among the prepared muffin cups, filling them about three-quarters full. Bake until a wooden skewer inserted into the center of a cupcake comes out clean, 20 to 24 minutes. Let the cupcakes cool in the pans on a wire rack for 10 minutes, then transfer them to the racks. Let cool completely.

TO MAKE THE FROSTING

3. In the bowl of a mixer fitted with the whisk attachment, beat the cream cheese, butter, and vanilla on medium-high speed until light and fluffy, about 2 minutes. Gradually beat in the sugar, and continue to mix until thoroughly combined, scraping down the sides of the bowl as needed. Use right away, or if the consistency is too soft, refrigerate the frosting until it is spreadable, about 15 minutes. The frosting will keep in the refrigerator for up to 3 days before using.

TO DECORATE THE CUPCAKES

4. Spread each cupcake with a thick layer of frosting, smoothing it as best you can. For each cupcake, add two regular chocolate chip eyes, a candy corn nose, and a wide mini chocolate chip mouth. Cut each sour strip crosswise into 4 thin strips for the brim of the hat, then cut the remaining in half crosswise then lengthwise to make a tall top hat. Arrange one brim above the eyes and insert the top hat into the frosting about the brim. Serve at once, or refrigerate for up to 2 days in an airtight container.

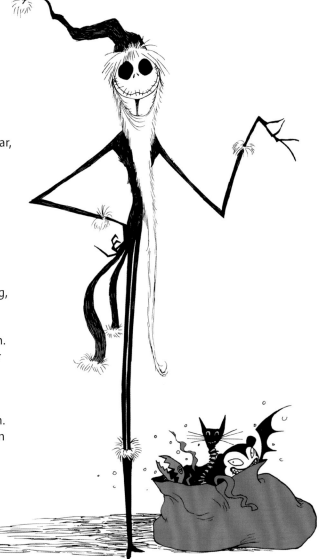

Sally Patchwork Layer Cake

Stitched together, with a penchant for potions, and a big heart, Sally is a beloved character in *The Nightmare Before Christmas*. Her iconic patchwork is re-created both in the interior and exterior here in this triple-layer cake worthy of any celebration.

Yield: 10 to 12 servings | Difficulty: Hard

FOR THE VANILLA CAKE

- 2¾ cups cake flour, plus more for dusting
- 1 tablespoon baking powder
- ½ teaspoon salt
- 1 cup (2 sticks) unsalted butter, cut into chunks, at room temperature, plus more for pans
- 1½ cups sugar
- 4 large whole eggs plus 2 large egg yolks
- 2 teaspoons vanilla extract
- 1 cup sour cream
- ⅛ teaspoon each dark pink, yellow, and teal gel food coloring

FOR THE DARK CHOCOLATE FROSTING

- 12 tablespoons (1½ sticks) unsalted butter, at cool room temperature
- 3 cups powdered sugar
- ¾ cup Dutch-process cocoa powder
- ½ cup whole milk
- 2 teaspoons vanilla extract
- ⅛ teaspoon salt

FOR THE VANILLA FROSTING

- 8 tablespoons (1 stick) unsalted butter, at cool room temperature
- 2½ cups powdered sugar
- 3 tablespoons whole milk
- 1 teaspoon vanilla extract
- Pinch of salt
- ⅛ teaspoon each dark pink, yellow, and teal gel food coloring

TO MAKE THE CAKE

1. Preheat the oven to 350°F. Butter the bottoms of three 9-inch round cake pans. Line with parchment paper. Lightly butter the parchment and sides of the pans and lightly dust with flour.

2. In a bowl, sift together the flour, baking powder, and salt. In the bowl of a mixer fitted with the paddle attachment, beat the butter and sugar on medium-high speed until fluffy. Add the whole eggs and yolks one at a time, beating well after each addition. Beat in the vanilla. Beating on low speed, add half the dry ingredients, and beat until just combined. Beat in the sour cream, and then the remaining dry ingredients, beating until just combined. The batter will be very thick.

3. Divide the batter among three bowls. Add pink food coloring to one bowl, yellow to the second bowl, and teal to the third bowl. Using a rubber spatula, gently stir the food coloring into each bowl of batter.

4. Spoon some of the pink batter into each prepared cake pan, then spoon some of the yellow batter into each pan, and then some of the teal batter. Repeat until the batter is evenly divided between the cake pans. Smooth the tops (they will slightly swirl together). Bake until a toothpick inserted into the center of the cakes comes out clean, 15 to 18 minutes. Let cool in the pans on wire racks for 15 minutes, then invert the cakes onto the racks, peel off the parchment, and let cool before frosting.

TO MAKE THE DARK CHOCOLATE FROSTING

5. In the bowl of a mixer fitted with the whisk attachment, beat the butter on medium speed until light and fluffy, about 1 minute. Sift the powdered sugar and cocoa into the bowl, then add the milk, vanilla, and salt. Mix on low speed just until combined. Scrape down the bowl with a rubber spatula. Beat on medium-high speed until the frosting is airy and smooth, about 2 minutes. Transfer ½ cup of the frosting to a small piping bag fitted with a ⅛-inch round tip; reserve for decorating the cake.

6. To frost the cake, place one layer, bottom side down, on a flat serving plate. If the cake top is slightly domed, carefully slice the dome off to level the cake and make a flat surface. With an icing spatula, spread the top with a medium-thick layer of frosting. Top with a second cake layer—level it as well, if needed—and top with a medium-thick layer of frosting. Top with the third cake layer, and level if needed or set the third layer bottom-side-up to create a flat surface. Cover the top and sides of the cake with a thin layer of the remaining frosting, spreading it as smoothly as possible to create a crumb coat to aid in frosting the rest of the cake. Refrigerate until the frosting is firm, at least 1 hour or up to 1 day in advance.

TO MAKE THE VANILLA FROSTING

7. In the bowl of a mixer fitted with the whisk attachment, beat the butter on medium speed until light and fluffy, about 1 minute. Sift the powdered sugar into the bowl, then add the milk, vanilla, and salt. Mix on low speed just until combined. Scrape down the bowl with a rubber spatula. Beat on medium-high speed until the frosting is airy and smooth, about 2 minutes. Divide the frosting among three bowls, and add one food coloring to each bowl. Stir each until well combined. Transfer each to a piping bag fitted with a ¼-inch round tip (you can do this one at a time if you don't have three bags and tips).

TO DECORATE THE CAKE

8. Outline patches, like Sally's dress, in different colors all over the cake, leaving some areas chocolate colored. Fill in the outlines with frosting of the same color, using a small offset spatula to gently spread the frosting to fill the patch. Use the reserved chocolate frosting to pipe stitching between the patches, swirls on the pink, and stripes and polka dots on the blue. Refrigerate for at least 1 hour to firm up the frosting; remove from the refrigerator at least 30 minutes before serving. The cake can be made up to 2 days in advance.

5

Drinks

Cucumber and Mint Limeade Love Potion

Vampire Brothers Bloody Party Punch

Witches Cauldron Brew

Homemade Christmas Eggnog

Halloween Town Band Zombie Mocktail

Frog's Breath Floats

Who in Halloween Town could possibly resist a cup of the Vampire Brothers' Bloody Party Punch or a glass of the Witches Cauldron Brew? Or even a sip of whatever the drink was that Sally bottled for Jack, which released a ghostly green butterfly when opened? (Maybe it was the Cucumber and Mint Limeade Love Potion offered here?) These custom-made concoctions will brighten up any bar, though be sure to stock up on sodas and juices for your less-brave guests. Suggestions to make boo-zy versions of these drinks are included for the adult guys and ghouls at your party.

Cucumber and Mint Limeade Love Potion

Shy Sally shows her affection for Jack by sending him a bottle of a green-hued potion that puffs into a butterfly when he opens it. You might not see butterflies, but this summery agua fresca will make you swoon. With flavors of cucumber, lime, and mint, it's a terrific addition to any outdoor party. For an adults-only version, add white tequila or rum.

Yield: 6 to 8 servings | Difficulty: Easy

- ¾ cup sugar
- Finely grated zest of 1 lime
- 1 cup fresh lime juice
- 1 large English cucumber, peeled
- ¼ cup fresh mint leaves
- 4 cups ice, or more as needed
- 2 cups (16 fluid ounces) sparkling water, chilled

1. In a saucepan over medium heat, combine 1 cup water, the sugar, and lime zest. Stir with a whisk until the sugar dissolves, about 2 minutes. Stir in the lime juice, remove from the heat, and let cool completely.

2. Halve the cucumber lengthwise and scoop out the seeds with a small spoon. Chop the cucumber and add to a blender along with the mint and the sugar mixture. Blend to a smooth purée.

3. Place a fine-mesh sieve over a bowl, and pour the mixture through the sieve. Use a rubber spatula to push the liquid through the sieve. Discard any solids. Transfer the mixture to a pitcher, and add the ice and sparkling water. Serve at once, adding more ice as needed.

Vampire Brothers Bloody Party Punch

The four Vampire Brothers of Halloween Town might be of different ranks, but they can all agree this is the punch for their party. The combination of blood orange and a whisper of vanilla transforms the blood-colored beverage into a simultaneously creamy and fruity treat. If you like, add a splash of vodka or rum for an adults-only version.

Yield: 10 to 12 servings | Difficulty: Easy

- One 10-ounce bag frozen strawberries
- 1 quart (32 fluid ounces) cranberry juice cocktail, chilled
- 1 teaspoon vanilla extract
- 3 cups ice cubes
- 2 cans (24 fluid ounces) blood orange soda, chilled
- 2 cups (16 fluid ounces) sparkling water, chilled

1. Add the strawberries, cranberry juice cocktail, and vanilla extract to a blender. Cover and blend on high speed to a smooth purée, about 2 minutes.

2. Pour the mixture into a punch bowl. Add the ice cubes, then add the orange soda and sparkling water. Stir gently to mix. Serve.

Witches Cauldron Brew

Using dry ice in a punch creates a dramatic bubbling cauldron effect and is a real showstopper. But use extreme caution when working with dry ice—make sure never to touch it with your bare skin or consume it. If you like, add a splash of vodka and some prosecco to the punch for an adults-only version.

Yield: 8 to 10 servings | Difficulty: Easy

- 1 quart (32 fluid ounces) unfiltered apple juice or cider, chilled
- 2 cans (24 fluid ounces) ginger beer, chilled
- 1 cup (8 fluid ounces) fresh orange juice, chilled
- ½ cup (4 fluid ounces) fresh lemon juice
- 4 cinnamon sticks
- 1 orange, halved lengthwise then thinly sliced crosswise
- 1 pound food-grade dry ice (optional) or 4 cups ice cubes

1. In a punch bowl, stir together the apple juice, ginger beer, orange juice, and lemon juice. Add the cinnamon sticks and orange slices.

2. If using the dry ice, use tongs to place the dry ice in the bottom of the punch bowl (do not touch the dry ice with your bare skin!). Use a ladle to serve the punch, avoiding anything that is still bubbling. Take extreme care not to ladle any of the dry ice into a cup.

3. If not using dry ice, add the ice cubes and serve.

Homemade Christmas Eggnog

There's no more festive holiday drink than a creamy, decadent cup of eggnog. This is a cooked version, so you don't have to worry about raw eggs. The addition of spirits will help the eggnog stay fresh for a few additional days, but feel free to leave it out.

Yield: 6 to 8 servings | Difficulty: Medium

- 3 cups (24 fluid ounces) whole milk
- 2 cups (16 fluid ounces) heavy cream, divided
- 6 large egg yolks
- ⅔ cup sugar
- 2 teaspoons vanilla extract
- ¼ teaspoon freshly grated nutmeg, plus more for garnish

1. In a saucepan over medium-low heat, warm the milk and 1 cup heavy cream until hot and steaming but not boiling, about 4 minutes. Meanwhile, in a heatproof bowl, whisk together the egg yolks and sugar until light in color, about 3 minutes.

2. While whisking constantly, slowly pour about half the milk mixture into the yolk mixture. Pour the yolk mixture back into the saucepan with the rest of the milk while continuing to whisk. Warm over low heat, whisking constantly, until the mixture simmers and thickens slightly, about 10 minutes; do not let the mixture boil. Add the vanilla and nutmeg, and whisk to combine. Transfer to an airtight container, and refrigerate until well chilled, preferably overnight but at least 2 hours.

3. In a medium bowl, beat the remaining 1 cup heavy cream to medium-stiff peaks. Gently fold into the eggnog mixture. Divide between 6 to 8 cups, and serve, garnished with additional nutmeg.

4. The eggnog will keep in an airtight container in the refrigerator for up to 2 days without alcohol or up to 1 week with alcohol.

Halloween Town Band Zombie Mocktail

The Halloween Town Band—James, Jimmy, and Jim—play saxophone, accordion, and stand-up bass and are seen often around town. This riff on a classic zombie cocktail is full of tropical flavor, and it just might inspire you to get up and dance. For an adults-only version, add rum to taste.

Makes 8 to 10 servings | Difficulty: Easy

- 1 quart (32 fluid ounces) pineapple juice, chilled
- 2 cups (16 fluid ounces) passion fruit juice or passion fruit and mango blend, chilled
- 1 cup (8 fluid ounces) fresh orange juice, chilled
- ½ cup (4 fluid ounces) fresh lemon juice
- ½ cup (4 fluid ounces) fresh lime juice
- 4 cups ice cubes

1. In a large serving pitcher, stir together pineapple juice, passion fruit juice, orange juice, lemon juice, and lime juice. Add ice and serve.

Frog's Breath Floats

Seeking freedom from Dr. Finkelstein, Sally uses Deadly Nightshade masked with frog's breath and worm's wort to render him unconscious when she wants to go out. These Frog's Breath Floats are perfectly safe, but beware! They might send you into a state of bliss. For an adults-only version, add a chocolate-mint liqueur.

Yield: 4 servings | Difficulty: Easy

FOR THE FLOATS
- 8 tablespoons chocolate syrup
- 2 cups (16 fluid ounces) club soda, chilled
- 8 scoops (about 1 quart) green mint chip ice cream
- Whipped cream store-bought or recipe below, for serving

FOR THE WHIPPED CREAM
- 1 cup cold heavy whipping cream
- ¼ cup sugar

1. Add 1 tablespoon chocolate syrup to each of four medium-tall glasses. Add ½ cup club soda to each glass, and gently stir until combined. Add two scoops ice cream to each glass, then drizzle each with 1 tablespoon chocolate syrup. Top with a dollop of whipped cream, and serve at once.

2. If making the whipped cream by hand, combine the heavy whipping cream and sugar in a bowl. Using a stand mixer fitted with a whisk attachment or an electric hand mixer, beat on high until stiff peaks form.

Measurement Conversion Charts

VOLUME

US	METRIC
⅕ teaspoon (tsp)	1 ml
1 teaspoon (tsp)	5 ml
1 tablespoon (tbsp)	15 ml
1 fluid ounce (fl. oz.)	30 ml
⅕ cup	50 ml
¼ cup	60 ml
⅓ cup	80 ml
3.4 fluid ounces (fl. oz.)	100 ml
½ cup	120 ml
⅔ cup	160 ml
¾ cup	180 ml
1 cup	240 ml
1 pint (2 cups)	480 ml
1 quart (4 cups)	.95 liter

TEMPERATURES

FAHRENHEIT	CELSIUS
200°	93.3°
212°	100°
250°	120°
275°	135°
300°	150°
325°	165°
350°	177°
400°	205°
425°	220°
450°	233°
475°	245°
500°	260°

WEIGHT

US	METRIC
0.5 ounce (oz.)	14 grams (g)
1 ounce (oz.)	28 grams (g)
¼ pound (lb.)	113 grams (g)
⅓ pound (lb.)	151 grams (g)
½ pound (lb.)	227 grams (g)
1 pound (lb.)	454 grams (g)

Notes

Parties

Is there anything better than gathering friends and family for a party with exciting games, great food and drink, lively conversation, and entertaining crafts amid bright and colorful decorations? There is when the party is *The Nightmare Before Christmas* themed! Tim Burton's classic holiday movie is all about designing a celebration that hits all the right notes.

Not everyone is a list maker like Santa Claus, but many of the decorations, crafts, and recipe components in the following parties can be made a few days in advance. There are also crafts for which the partygoer needs to provide an item—for example, a four-by-six photo of themselves for the Christmas Party's Christmas/Halloween Photo Mash-Up. Note this on the invitation, along with a request for your guests to dress up as their favorite character. And after the party, remember to email photos to your partygoers!

Parties are about having fun and, like Jack, making the occasion your own. Have a thought for a game or craft not suggested here? Want to decorate your Birthday Party with ideas from the Christmas Party? Feel free to mix and match any element, as they all celebrate Jack, Sally, Zero, and Santa Claus's efforts to create the best holiday festivities ever.

Online Resources

Throughout these parties, you'll find a number of templates you can access from our online resource web page. When you see this symbol ⬇, it means there is a downloadable element you can access from this website: insighteditions.com/NightmareEntertaining

"This Is Halloween" Party

INVITATION
Monster Under the Bed Invitation

DECOR
Full Moon and Halloween Town Shadows
"This Is Halloween" Banner
Halloween Countdown Clock
Black-Light Bugs, Spiders, and Scorpions
Glow-in-the-Dark Pumpkin Heads

CRAFTS AND FAVORS
Oogie Boogie Deck of Cards
Vampire Protection Parasols
The Mayor Hat and Badge
The Mayor Mood-Changing Mask
Lock, Shock, and Barrel Papier-Mâché Masks

ACTIVITIES
Trick-or-Treating With Lock, Shock, and Barrel
Clawfoot Bathtub Race
Halloween Town Costume Contest
Dodge the Sunlight Vampire Game
Jack the Pumpkin King Pumpkin-Carving Contest

MENU

"This Is Halloween" Party

Once their work for the Halloween holiday is complete, the citizens of Halloween Town celebrate with singing, dancing, and gathering together in the town square. As the Corpse Kid and the Withered Winged Demon sing in "This Is Halloween," "Life's no fun without a good scare," and we agree. There's candy to eat, costumes to dress up in, and trick-or-treating to do. Best of all is doing these things with friends who share your love for chills, thrills, and the peculiar population of Halloween Town.

The frights begin with a foreboding invitation featuring the Monster Under the Bed beckoning guests to join in. Decorations evoke the delightfully dark community of Halloween Town, filled with shadows and spirits, illuminated by a full moon and pumpkins that blaze with a fiery light. There's no mistaking what holiday is being celebrated with a "This Is Halloween" banner draped at an entrance or within your party space.

The Mayor of Halloween Town may be two-faced, but he truly cares about his ghoulish charges. You can elect one of your partygoers to help with official duties by wearing the Mayor's hat and badge—or wear these yourself in your role as host. There's also a two-sided Mayor's mask craft that displays his ever-changing moods. With him, it's either joyous confidence or frantic dismay.

Items from Oogie Boogie's lit-up lair, such as glow-in-the dark playing cards and dice, serve as a reminder that even in Halloween Town there are beings that give its citizens nightmares. Oogie's minions—Lock, Shock, and Barrel—are pretty nightmarish themselves, but crafting papier-mâché masks of the tiny trio is a trick-or-treater's dream.

The masks and parasols also figure into suggested games for the party. Trick-or-treating with Lock, Shock, and Barrel features a scavenger hunt for candy. Partygoers can race miniature versions of the walking clawfoot tub to see who can get to Christmas Town faster. Wannabe vampires join in the fun when guests must use their parasols to avoid being exposed to the light. Traditional Halloween amusements get a *Nightmare* upgrade, with a pumpkin-carving competition that celebrates the Pumpkin King. And it isn't Halloween without a costume contest! Encourage your guests to dress up like Halloween Town characters. Glowing jack-o'-lanterns and bugs, a full moon, and to-die-for cuisine will make this the most "horrible" Halloween party yet!

Monster Under the Bed Invitation

The invitation to your *Nightmare Before Christmas Halloween* celebration offers a scare before the party even starts: Your invitees will have to brave looking under the bed to find the details. The glowing red eyes and nasty sharp teeth of the monster will make everybody scream—with delight, of course.

- Monster Under the Bed Invitation template ⬇
- Printer
- White printer paper
- Pencil
- Scissors
- Black card stock
- White or solid-colored paper
- Patterned paper featuring plaid, stripes, dots, or other designs
- Glue
- Lace or ruffled ribbon
- Red glitter, sequins, or jewels
- White or silver permanent marker
- Cotton balls or white card stock

1. Create the invite's bed frame shape by downloading the template from our Online Resources ⬇. Print on white printer paper, cut it out, and trace the shape on the black card stock. Cut it out.

2. Cut a white piece of paper that covers the entire card except for the bed's headboard and footboard. This is the bedsheets.

3. Cut the patterned paper into a slightly more squared piece that fits over the white paper, but leave about a half inch of white visible on the left for the sheets. This is your bed's blanket.

4. Glue the top half-inch of the patterned paper to the white sheet. Let dry, then glue the top half-inch of the white paper to the top of the bed frame to create the card. Cut the lace or ribbon for a dust ruffle, and glue it to the bottom of the paper blanket.

5. Once dry, open the card. With white or silver permanent marker, draw a grinning mouthful of pointy teeth on one side of the invitation. Outline two eyes above the mouth, then glue red glitter, sequins, or jewels (or all three!) to make the monster's eyeballs.

6. Write down the party details next to the monster with the white marker. To cut down on writing time, you can type up the details (in a chilling font), print out, and glue to the inside of the card.

7. Close the card, and glue cotton balls or white card stock cut into a rectangle to the headboard side of the front to make a pillow.

Full Moon and Halloween Town Shadows

Shadows seep into every corner of Halloween Town, made even darker against the light of a full moon. And what lurks within the moon's gloom? Wicked black cats, flapping bats, and perhaps a skull or two. Decorating your party space with these iconic images will make Jack Skellington feel right at home.

- Shadow templates ⊙
- Printer
- White printer paper
- Pencil
- Black card stock or paper
- Large piece of gold paper or gold poster board

- Scissors
- Masking tape or painter's tape
- Hole punch (optional)
- String or monofilament (optional)
- Removable nonpermanent hooks (optional)
- Flashlight (optional)

1. Download the templates from our Online Resources page ⊙, print onto white printer paper, and cut out. Trace onto black card stock, and cut out. Alternatively, draw your own cats, bats, spiders, trees, haunted houses, or skulls, and cut them out of the black card stock.

2. To make the full moon, trace a large circle on the gold paper or poster board, and cut out.

3. Create a loop with the masking tape or painter's tape by attaching the tape to itself with the sticky side facing out. Use these loops to tape the shadows to your walls and windows.

4. To hang shapes from your ceiling, punch a small hole in the top of the shadowy silhouettes, and hang them with string or monofilament using removable nonpermanent hooks.

5. You can also create a shadow projection with a flashlight. Measure the diameter of your flashlight head and cut out a few shadows out of black card stock that will fit the flashlight head. Tape the shadow on and point the flashlight at a wall or the ceiling to project the shadow's shape on the wall. The closer the flashlight is to the wall, the more distinct the shape is. The farther away the wall is, the less distinct the edges will be.

"This Is Halloween" Banner

Surrounded by black-light bugs and grinning pumpkins, is there any doubt your guests will know this party is all about Halloween? Probably not, but proclaim it loudly in the form of a banner based on the iconic opening song of *The Nightmare Before Christmas*! Sheet music creates the perfect backdrop for each letter in the banner.

- "This Is Halloween" Banner template ⬇
- Printer
- White paper or old sheet music
- Hole punch
- Scissors
- Twine

1. Download the templates from our Online Resources page ⬇. Print each letter and icon on an individual sheet of paper or on a piece of sheet music. You can scale the letters down to fit two per sheet depending on the size of banner you'd like to have.

2. Using the hole punch, punch a hole in the top corner of each piece of paper, and thread the twine through the holes. You can make one long banner, or split it into two banners and have "This Is" above "Halloween" on the bottom. Leave extra twine on the ends, and hang in a doorway, archway, across an opening, or across windows.

3. You can embellish the banner by hanging other elements from the party, such as the black-light bugs or cutout shadows. Fake spiderwebs and string lights add even more fright.

DEC JAN FEB MAR APR MAY JUN JUL AUG SEP OCT NOV
035
DAYS TO HAL
XMAS

Halloween Countdown Clock

To keep on top of the Halloween schedule, Halloween Town displays a clock that counts down the days until the holiday, set high on Town Hall in the center of the metropolis. Use this clock to count down the days until it's time to celebrate the spookiest day of the year—or to remind you of the number of days until your party.

- Wooden circular clock face
- Clock kit
- Black permanent marker
- White chalk marker
- Small rectangular wooden sign
- Small square wooden sign
- Small wood sign with chalk front
- Metal brads
- Brown moss
- Hot glue
- White, red and black paint
- Paintbrushes
- String or twine

1. For the clock, paint the clock face white and allow to dry. Using the black paint or marker, add a spiderweb shape to the front of the clock. Write the months around the outside of the clock face. Using the hot glue, glue the moss around the edge of the clock. Follow the directions of the clock kit to add the clock hands and mechanism to the clock. Hang the clock on the wall.

2. For the countdown, use the small wood sign with chalk front. Add metal brads around the outside edge to replicate screws. Using the chalk marker, write the number of days until Halloween or Christmas. Hang on the wall below the clock.

3. For the "days to halloween" sign, paint the small rectangular wooden sign white and allow to dry. Using the black paint or marker, write "DAYS TO HALLOWEEN" on the sign. Hang on the wall below the countdown.

4. For the "xmas" sign use the small square wooden sign. Using the red paint, add "XMAS" to the sign. Glue string or twine to the back of the sign to make a hanger. Attach the string to the back of the "days to halloween" sign covering up "halloween" to switch the clock from a Halloween countdown to a Christmas countdown.

Black-Light Bugs, Spiders, and Scorpions

The Mad Scientist Dr. Finkelstein might be able to enlighten us on why anything coated with fluorescent paint can be seen under black light. However, it's a lot more fun just to enjoy the eerie radiance of this horde of creepy-crawlies.

- Cardboard or newspaper (a generous amount)
- Plastic beetles, centipedes, worms, spiders, and scorpions
- Fluorescent spray paint in several colors
- Black-light bulbs

1. Cover a surface outdoors with cardboard or newspaper.

2. Spread out the plastic bugs on the cardboard or newspaper in a single layer.

3. Using different colors on different bugs, paint them with the florescent spray paint.

4. Allow to dry completely, and then set them on tables, your table scape, the floor, or any other surface where guests might encounter them.

5. Place black-light bulbs in light fixtures around the party space to make the bugs shine. To get an even brighter gleam, lower window blinds or close drapes to reduce the amount of daylight coming in, or turn off the room's white lights.

Glow-in-the-Dark Pumpkin Heads

It's not shocking that the sign pointing to Halloween Town is a representation of the Pumpkin King's fiery and toothy grin. Pay tribute to the Pumpkin King with these radiant jack-o'-lanterns, sure to light up your party with fiendish glee.

- Cardboard or newspaper
- Several real or fake pumpkins, uncarved
- Black-light paint or glow-in-the-dark paint in several different colors
- Paintbrushes
- Black-light bulbs

1. Spread cardboard or newspaper on an outdoor surface.

2. Using black-light or glow-in-the-dark paint, decorate each pumpkin with different jack-o'-lantern faces. If you want to get fancy, paint the faces of Jack or Sally or any other Nightmare character on the pumpkins. Allow to dry.

3. Place the pumpkins near your front door, on the front porch, or on a walkway leading up to the party. Be sure to replace the front porch bulb and any other outdoor lighting with black-light bulbs to make sure the faces glow!

Crafts

Oogie Boogie Deck of Cards

Oogie Boogie's lair is a glowing gambling den filled with one-armed bandits that really shoot and a deck of enormous playing cards that brandish whirling knives. Creating a version of Oogie's cards is deadly fun, and you can use these cards in a few games or as decor for the party—string the cards up like a garland, stick them on walls, or place them on tables and set up a few black lights around the room. Add a set of luminous dice and make an Oogie Boogie–style casino.

You can also turn this into an activity: while guests are still arriving, leave the deck of cards out for people to paint as the party is getting started, then let them dry. Later during the party you can mix the cards together and turn on a black light for some fun games!

- Standard deck of playing cards
- Invisible black-light paint
- Paintbrushes
- Black light

1. Using black-light paint, decorate the card faces with Oogie Boogie–approved images, such as snakes, worms, beetles, spiders, stitches, and even Oogie Boogie's face. Be sure to paint only the faces of the cards and leave the backs clean. Allow to dry.

2. As black-light paint is invisible in white light, the seemingly "normal" decks of cards turn into a more sinister game when a black light is turned on and the creatures painted on the cards come alive!

Vampire Protection Parasols

When Jack cannot be found after Halloween, the four Vampire Brothers wait outside his gates before dawn, expressing worry at his disappearance. Once the sun rises, they must use their capes to shield themselves from the light. Things would have been easier if they had remembered to bring their black parasols for protection. Here's a way to express your inner bloodsucker, by making a personalized parasol.

- Paper or silk parasols (at least one per guest)
- Stickers, paint, paintbrushes, glitter, ribbon, cobwebs, plastic insects, spiders, bats, and snakes
- Hot glue
- Monofilament
- Scissors

1. Purchase inexpensive paper or silk parasols in black, white, green, orange, or purple, enough for each vampire—uh, guest.

2. Put together a station for partygoers to personalize their vampire sun protection that offers stickers, paints, glitter, ribbon, cobwebs, and plastic critters.

3. Hot-glue decorations to fabric or hang them off the ribs of the parasol using monofilament.

4. Personalize your parasol by adding your vampire name. Hang onto it for protection against the sun, and for the Dodge the Sunlight Vampire Game.

The Mayor Hat and Badge

"Great Halloween, everyone!" the Mayor tells the townspeople. And he can't wait for the next one—but needs Jack's help. However, Jack has disappeared, so the Mayor decides to sound the alarm. "I'm only an elected official here," he exclaims. "I can't make decisions by myself!" But decisions will have to be made—the first being who will be favored with the Mayor's hat and badge.

FOR THE BADGE

- White paper or white sticker
- Scissors
- Black first place ribbon
- Black permanent marker
- Glue

1. Cut the white paper or sticker in a circle big enough to cover the center of the black ribbon.

2. Write "MAYOR" on the paper or sticker in black permanent marker.

3. Place the sticker or glue the paper on the center of the ribbon.

FOR THE HAT

- Two pieces of black poster board (each at least 2 feet wide)
- Scissors
- Glue
- Black tape (optional)
- Gray ribbon
- Black elastic
- Hole punch

1. Cut a large circle from one piece of the black poster board approximately 2 feet in diameter.

2. Roll the second piece of poster board into a tube on the long side to create the Mayor's hat's signature height. Glue or use black tape on the seam to keep the tube closed.

3. Once dry, glue the tube to the center of the circle. If easier, make four or five snips around the bottom of the tube and fold these up to make tabs. Glue the tabs onto the circle so the tube is centered. Don't worry about seeing the tabs—they will be covered.

4. Wrap the gray ribbon around the base where the tube meets the circle of the hat, then glue in place. Cut off any excess ribbon.

5. To make a chin strap, punch a small hole on opposite sides of the hat and thread the elastic through the holes. Tie a knot on one end of the elastic large enough so the elastic won't slip through, and put on the hat to measure how long the chin strap should be, using yourself as the model. Pull the unknotted side of the elastic up through its hole, and knot it off. Cut off any excess elastic above the knot. Make sure it fits well—you don't want the hat slipping off!

6. Award the hat and the ribbon to the Mayor of the party, perhaps by lottery or to the winner of a game.

The Mayor Mood-Changing Mask

There is no doubt what the Mayor is feeling at any given time—he either beams with a confident smile or demonstrates dismay with a toothy frown, and there's little in between. Make this mood-changing mask, and you can be as two-faced as he is.

- White card stock
- Peach card stock
- Scissors
- Markers in black, red, and yellow
- Glue
- Wooden ice-pop stick or tongue depressor
- Two pieces of black poster board

1. Stack the white card stock and peach card stock, and cut an oval large enough to cover a face.

2. On the peach-colored oval, create the happy face of the Mayor. Using the black marker, draw two ovals for eyes: one blue-filled (the left) and one with a swirl (the right) topped by half-circle eyebrows. He has a long teardrop shaped nose, with the right half filled in black, and a wide red mouth. Don't forget to draw little red circles for his blushing cheeks.

3. On the white-colored oval, draw his angry face: two egg-shaped yellow eyes with black pupils, and diagonal lines for eyebrows. He has a black upside-down crescent for a nose and a huge unhappy mouth filled with jagged teeth.

4. Sandwich the two faces together, back to back, with the wooden stick in the middle and sticking out the bottom. Glue everything together.

5. For the Mayor's hat, stack two pieces of black poster board together, and cut out the shape of a tall rectangle atop a slightly shorter rectangle shape, at right angles to each other. Separate the pieces, and glue one hat to the top of each face, then glue the hats together at the top. Allow to dry.

6. Use your switchable mood-changing mask to express your mayoral feelings during the party.

7. You can also leave the hat off one double-sided face for the wearer of The Mayor Hat and Badge (page 124) to use during the party instead.

Lock, Shock, and Barrel Papier-Mâché Masks

Lock, Shock, and Barrel are Oogie's masked imps: Lock wears a devil mask, Shock wears a green witch's mask, and Barrel, a white ghoul mask, almost a childish version of Jack Skellington's face. Oddly, when they remove their masks, they pretty much look the same!

- Newspaper
- Bowl and whisk
- Flour
- Water
- Scissors or precision knife
- Cardboard
- Glue
- 3 plastic full-face masks
- Cooking oil or cooking spray (optional)
- Paint and paintbrushes
- Permanent markers

1. Tear up the newspaper into small pieces and strips.

2. Mix 1 cup flour and 2 cups water (those are the proportions to follow if you need to make more). Stir until all the lumps are gone.

3. For Lock's mask, cut two devilish horn shapes from the cardboard and glue to the top of the mask. Alternatively, you can cut horn shapes on the mask itself (as long as it will still cover most of the wearer's face).

4. For Shock's mask, cut a long, large nose from the cardboard and glue on.

5. For Barrel's mask, don't do anything! Keep as is.

6. If you want to remove the papier-mâché-formed mask from the original mask form, cover the mask forms with a light coat of cooking oil or cooking spray. You can also leave the papier-mâché on the original masks.

7. Dip the newspaper pieces into the flour mixture until wet. Cover the mask forms completely with overlapping pieces of newspaper, but be sure to leave the eyes and mouth holes uncovered. Allow to dry overnight.

8. For Lock: Paint the mask red, and add a toothy, devilish smile.

9. For Shock: Paint the mask green with small eyes and a frown.

10. For Barrel: Paint the mask white, and add a skeleton's smile, large round eyes, and two small lines for nasal bones.

11. Use as decorations for the party or as a mask for your costume. If you left the papier-mâché on the original mask, just use the existing elastic band. If you removed the papier-mâché mask from the plastic mask, cut a small hole around the temple of your mask and attach a piece of elastic to hold the mask in place.

Trick-or-Treating With Lock, Shock, and Barrel

While Santa Claus goes over his list of who's naughty and who's nice, the unquestioningly naughty Lock, Shock, and Barrel arrive. The trio kidnap the jolly gift-giver, stuff him in a bag, and drag him to Halloween Town to discover his holiday has been hijacked by Jack Skellington. To sweeten the blow, how about a good, old-fashioned hunt for candy?

- Individually wrapped candy
- Bowls, baskets, cauldrons, or any kind of spooky vessel

1. Encourage your guests to wear a costume and bring something to put candy in, like their own plastic cauldron or jack-o'-lantern basket. Three guests can wear the Lock, Shock, and Barrel Papier-Mâché Masks (page 126).

2. If you're playing with children, place containers of candy all over the party space. Some in obvious places, like the food table, and others in places they'll have to find, such as under the bed, on the stairs, in closets, outside, etc. If you're hosting a party for adults, make them work a little for it! Hide full-sized candy in clever spaces for them to find.

3. Encourage your guests to yell "trick-or-treat" every time they find candy and to look for as much as they can.

Clawfoot Bathtub Race

There are several unique forms of transportation in Halloween Town. The Mayor drives his hearse, and Jack rides a snowmobile or flies a coffin sleigh. But perhaps the most unexpected vehicle is the walking clawfoot bathtub that Lock, Shock, and Barrel use to capture Sandy Claws. Race your own version of the terrible tricksters' favorite conveyance with these mini clawfoot tubs.

- Two mini clawfoot bathtub soap dishes or two DIY versions
- Large sheet of black cardboard or foam poster board
- Permanent markers

1. Yes, you can actually purchase mini clawfoot tubs, which are used to hold soap, small toiletries, and even small plants. Or you can make your own little bathtubs out of clay or paper cups or bowls. Don't forget to add the feet!

2. Using the large sheet of cardboard and markers, draw a racecourse background for the tubs. Decorate by drawing scenery that Lock, Shock, and Barrel might see along the way, for instance, a pumpkin patch, pet cemetery, or haunted forest.

3. Set up the racetrack by propping the cardboard against a wall at an angle—around 45 degrees. Secure the course in place with books or bricks on the bottom corners of the cardboard, but make sure there is plenty of space in the middle for the two racing cars to speed through.

4. Number the bathtubs 1 and 2 with the permanent markers. Or name them Lock and Shock, if you like.

5. Have two guests hold the tubs at the top of the cardboard, count down to one, at which point the guest will release their tub, allowing it to race down the course—the tub that goes the fastest or the farthest wins!

Halloween Town Costume Contest

Of course, the citizens of Halloween Town don't think they're wearing costumes! A striped suit with black bat tie, a patchwork dress, and a Mad Scientist's lab coat are just daily fare for them. For non-Halloween Town residents, one of the best aspects of this holiday is dressing up as your favorite ghoul, bogeyman, or skeleton. Even more fun is having a judge determine "who wore it best" and designate the most outstanding attire as the new Pumpkin King. You can congratulate the winner with a "Nice work, Bone Daddy!"

- Black card stock
- Scissors
- Glue
- Gold trophy cup(s)
- Black permanent marker

1. Cut two bat wings from the black card stock, and glue one to each handle of the gold trophy. You can also cut out a smiling jack-o'-lantern, or even Jack's face, and glue that to the front of the trophy cup.

2. Use the marker to inscribe "Pumpkin King" on the base. You can make additional trophies for second and third place with kudos like "SQUASHED IT" or "GOURD JOB."

3. Have guests come in costume, and appoint a judge.

4. During the party, have the judge pick the best costume, and have a small ceremony to award the winner the trophy. The winner is the new Pumpkin King!

5. You can make multiple trophies for Sally, Zero, Oogie Boogie, and so on!

Dodge the Sunlight Vampire Game

One of the awards at the Mayor's Halloween Town celebration goes to the Vampires for "Most Blood Drained in a Single Evening." The four Vampire Brothers are on the job 24-7, so in daytime, they carry large black parasols to keep them safe from the sunlight. To play this game, your guests will become creatures of the night and scurry to avoid the sunlight's glare.

- Vampire Protection Parasols (page 122), or any parasols or umbrellas you may have at home

- Flashlight

1. Choose the first person who will be "It" to start the game. They get the flashlight.

2. Give each vampire—er, guest—a parasol or umbrella, or have them use their personalized parasol from the craft on page 122.

3. In the darkness outside, have "It" use the flashlight to aim a ray of sunshine at the vampires.

4. The vampires need to protect themselves from the sun using their parasols.

5. If a vampire is hit with a beam of sunlight from the knees or above, they become the next "It"!

Jack the Pumpkin King Pumpkin-Carving Contest

Jack-o'-lanterns have been part of Halloween celebrations for centuries. There's no denying the expression on Jack the Pumpkin King's face could "make wounds ooze and flesh crawl!" as the Undersea Gal describes it, but we think his smile really brings cheer rather than fear. Carve out a place for the results among your decor after the competition, then send everyone home with a grinning souvenir.

- Newspaper-covered carving surface
- Bowls for pumpkin seeds, pulp, and pumpkin chunks
- Pumpkin-carving knives and spoons (at least one per guest or per team of two guests)
- Markers (one for each pumpkin)
- Paper towels
- Several real carving pumpkins (at least one per guest or team)
- Tea candles
- Matches or lighter

1. On a solid surface covered with layers of newspaper, set out bowls, pumpkin-carving knives and spoons, and markers. You'll also need to have paper towels close at hand because it's going to get messy!

2. Give each guest a pumpkin, or have them team up in twos. Guests can also bring their own pumpkin if they haven't gotten to carving it yet!

3. Have each guest or team remove the top of the pumpkin and empty out the seeds and pulp first.

4. Next, instruct each guest or team to carve Jack's face into the pumpkin (have an image or two of Jack wearing different expressions nearby for reference). To make things difficult, rules can be made, such as drawing the initial outline of Jack's face blindfolded.

5. The guest or team who carves the best version of Jack's face becomes Mayor and is awarded The Mayor Hat and Badge from page 124.

6. Place a tea candle in each pumpkin and light them to enjoy their glowing visages during the party.

Menu

SNACKS

STARTERS

ENTRÉES

SIDES

DESSERTS

- Jack Skellington White Chocolate Skull Bowls With Chocolate Mousse (page 82)

DRINKS

- Witches Cauldron Brew (page 104)

The Nightmare Before Christmas Party

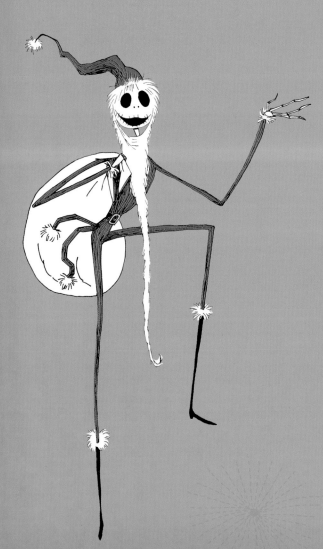

INVITATION
Christmas Card Ransom-Note Invitation

DECOR
Spooky Wreaths and Garlands

Christmas Tree With Creepy Ornaments and Giant Snake Garland

Christmas Lights Electric Chair

Spiderweb Spiral of Christmas Lights

Spider Paper Chain

Scary Snowman

CRAFTS AND FAVORS
The Nightmare Before Christmas Ornaments

Sandy Claws Hats and Soul-Taking Stockings

Dreadful Snow Globes

Christmas/Halloween Photo Mash-Up

ACTIVITIES
House of Christmas Cards

White Elephant Gift-Giving Game

Halloween Town Christmas Carols

The Nightmare Before Christmas Creature Creator

MENU

The Nightmare Before Christmas Party

Following his visit to Christmas Town, Jack Skellington discovers he loves the holiday, though he still finds it confusing and elusive. Obsessed with putting some logic to it, he conducts a series of experiments and comes to the revelation that though he cannot see what the holiday means, he can believe in it. And then, eureka! He believes he can make an even better job of it. Jack employs the residents of Halloween Town to make Christmas theirs. Making your Christmas party the Halloween Town way will bring about festivities that are equally memorable.

Every party starts with an invitation—and this one cannot be ignored. It's a ransom note proclaiming Santa Claus has been kidnapped, so guests should arrive ready to have some holiday fun before he's "released."

The traditional wreaths and garlands of this winter holiday are given the Halloween Town treatment by replacing sparkling ornaments and silver bells with spiders, eyeballs, and rats. And there's no Christmas without a decorated tree: for this occasion, choose black and orange ribbons, spiderwebs, bats, and bones, with an orange-and-black-striped snake for draping around the trunk.

Wrap lights around an electric chair or spiral them inside a spider's web to add that special Christmas glow; festoon doorways and windows with spider paper chains, and build some very sinister snowmen to greet your guests with eyes as black and fearsome as Jack's. Your guests will be able to personalize their own Sandy Claws hats to wear during the party along with other clever crafts. Note that the *The Nightmare Before Christmas* Ornaments (page 146) need a bit of time to cure, so plan accordingly!

Christmas isn't Christmas without gifts! The presents received in the White Elephant Gift-Giving Game shouldn't be gross, but they should be terrible. And like Jack, you can build a house made of Christmas cards, but this time it's a competition to see who can build a tower tall enough to rival the home of the Pumpkin King.

With songs and games and lights and gifts, how horrible—no, how jolly!—this Christmas Party will be.

Christmas Card Ransom-Note Invitation

Jack assigns Lock, Shock, and Barrel—Oogie Boogie's sidekicks—to kidnap Sandy Claws as he's putting together his Christmas makeover. This invitation, in the manner of a ransom note, will do the trick to entreat your guests. If they will be crafting the Christmas/Halloween Photo Mash-Up, remember to include additional details on the invite for your guests to bring a four-by-six photo of themselves.

- One or more magazines you're willing to cut up
- Scissors
- Glue
- White card stock or other colored card stock
- Copier (or scanner and printer)
- Manila envelopes

1. Find and cut out individual letters in the magazine(s) to spell "WE HAVE KIDNAPPED SANTA CLAWS" and glue onto the card stock.

2. Write in the party's details below that (including anything the guests need to bring), and make as many copies as needed. You can also scan in the ransom letter and type the additional details. Print out as many copies as you need from the scanned version.

3. Send the invitation in a plain manila envelope to make an even more authentic-looking ransom note.

Decor

Spooky Wreaths and Garlands

When Jack returns from Christmas Town, he decorates his home with elements of his newly discovered holiday by hanging festoons of ornamental greenery around his laboratory and installing a spindly tree in his bedroom. The rest of the denizens of Halloween Town join in with their own ideas of yuletide decor, including dyeing wreaths decorated with tiny skulls. Bring Halloween Town's special look of Christmas to your party with these spooky wreaths and garlands.

- Green or black fake garlands
- Green or black fake wreaths
- Orange or black spray paint (optional)
- Christmas ornaments
- Christmas lights
- Plastic or rubber eyeballs, fangs, rats, spiders, spiderwebs, skeleton hands, bones, etc.
- Black or orange ribbon
- Christmas ribbon
- White, yellow, and black felt
- Wire
- Hot glue
- White poster board (optional)
- Measuring tape (optional)
- Pencil (optional)

1. First, figure out where garlands and wreaths can be hung or draped in your home to determine how much you will need. These can go on doors, windows, walls, banisters, mantels, or railings.

2. You can keep them the traditional black or green (the way you bought them), or add a touch of orange or black with spray paint, and allow to dry. Once dry, hang in your desired spots.

3. Time to decorate! First add Christmas lights to the garlands. Then mix traditional Christmas ornaments with Halloween-centric decor such as eyeballs, fangs, rats, spiders, spiderwebs, skeleton hands, and bones, then add ribbons as needed to fill in any other spaces.

4. Optional: You can make some garlands or wreaths seem as if they're coming alive by adding faces, or fake arms or hands. To make a replica of the Man-Eating Wreath from the movie, use one large round green wreath and affix thin garlands to each side to create the arms. Cut out two large eyes from the yellow felt, and cut two small black circles from the black felt for the pupils. Cut out pointy, triangular teeth from the white felt. Attach the eyes and teeth with hot glue, making sure to hot-glue the teeth to the back of the wreath so they are visible from the front.

Christmas Tree With Creepy Ornaments and Giant Snake Garland

The door to Christmas Town twinkles with glittery ornaments, candy canes, and red trains, though this is not at all what Jack would have for his version of the holiday! His Christmas is filled with bats, shrunken heads, and a large orange-and-black-striped snake that winds around a Christmas tree in the real world (and then tries to eat the tree!). With his Halloween makeover, Christmas is his. And now, it's yours!

FOR THE CHRISTMAS TREE

- Real or fake Christmas tree in green or black, in a stand
- Spray paint (optional)
- Christmas lights
- Black and orange ribbons or beaded garlands
- Traditional Christmas ornaments and decor
- Plastic eyeballs, fangs, rats, spiders, spiderwebs, skeleton hands, bones, etc.
- *The Nightmare Before Christmas* Ornaments (page 146) or similar

TO MAKE THE CHRISTMAS TREE

1. Whether you choose a real or fake Christmas tree, you can add touches of orange and black to it with spray paint if you like. Just be sure to spray paint outside or in a well-ventilated area and allow the paint to dry completely before going to the next steps.

2. Get your Christmas tree in place to decorate! Add traditional Christmas lights, ribbons, and ornaments to give it a most festive look.

3. Then add some nontraditional embellishments: eyeballs, fangs, rats, spiders, spiderwebs instead of tinsel, skeleton hands, bones, etc. You can also hang your own *The Nightmare Before Christmas* Ornament on it.

FOR THE SNAKE GARLAND

- Orange-and-black-striped opaque tights, long socks, or fabric
- Scissors
- Needle and thread
- Stuffing (cotton or wool batting will work)
- Hot glue
- Googly or jiggly craft eyes
- White felt
- Red felt or ribbon

TO MAKE THE SNAKE GARLAND

1. If using striped tights, cut off each leg of the tights. You can make two snake garlands out of a pair of tights. If using fabric, roll into a tube 2 to 3 inches in diameter. Stitch the long sides together, then sew one end shut.

2. Fill the tights, socks, or fabric tube snake with stuffing, and be sure to stuff one end with slightly more stuffing for the head. Sew the second end shut.

3. Use hot glue to attach googly eyes to one end of the snake to create the head. Cut two small pieces of white felt into triangles, and hot-glue to the front for fangs. Hot-glue a small piece of red felt or red ribbon for the tongue. Cut a small triangle from the end of the ribbon to create a forked tongue.

4. Drape the snake on the floor in a spiral around the tree.

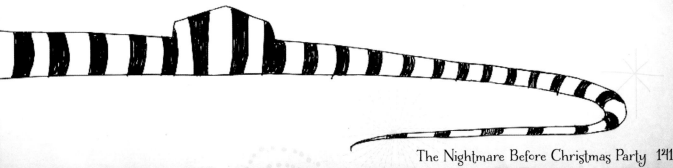

Christmas Lights Electric Chair

Jack realizes Christmas shouldn't be tricky; it should be fun! And he can even improve it with Halloween Town's kind of fun. Putting his ideas into action, he pulls the colored lights from the pitiful tree he's put up and coils them around an electric chair—just the first of many bright ideas.

- Measuring tape
- Chair with a back
- Old metal colander
- Saw
- 2-by-4-inch piece of lumber
- Drill and screws
- Black painter's tape or masking tape for easy removal, or duct tape for a stronger hold.
- Strands of multicolored Christmas lights

1. Measure the height from the floor to the top of a willing participant's head—ideally this person will roughly be the size of the average party attendee—while they sit in the chair, then add the height of the colander. Cut the lumber to the measured height, or have it cut at your local lumber store when you purchase it.

2. Place the colander upside down on the top of the wood and attach using the drill and screws. Tape the board with the colander to the back of the chair, so the colander sticks up and over the seat.

3. Wrap the Christmas lights around the legs and back of the chair, and up and around the colander. Avoid placing lights on the seat of the chair!

4. Darken the room and plug in the lights for an electrifying decoration.

Spiderweb Spiral of Christmas Lights

Among the earliest decorations Jack puts up in his tower after returning from Christmas Town is a circle of multicolored lights that spiral out from the center of a large spiderweb. Here's an easy way to display your traditional Christmas lights with the Pumpkin King's flair. This decoration works well on a large window or wall.

- Three short strands of Christmas lights or LED string lights
- One long strand of Christmas lights or LED string lights
- Thumbtacks or tape
- Zip ties

1. Using two of the short strands of lights, form an X, and attach it to a wall or window with thumbtacks or tape. With the third short strand of lights, make a vertical line down through the X, and attach. Make sure you have the end with the plug on it facing toward the ground.

2. Attach the end of the long strand of lights that does not have the plug to the center of the X with a zip tie. Then wind the lights outward in a circle. Wherever the long strand meets a short strand, attach together with a zip tie. Continue in a spiral shape until the spiderweb is complete.

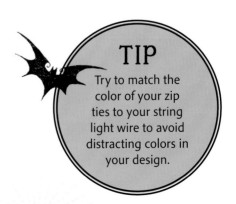

TIP

Try to match the color of your zip ties to your string light wire to avoid distracting colors in your design.

Spider Paper Chain

Desperate to find a "logical way to explain this Christmas thing," Jack runs a series of tests based on the scientific method. For one experiment, he carefully follows instructions on how to cut out a paper snowflake. But to his consternation, the cuts he makes reveal a spider when the paper is unfolded. The spiders in this paper chain are cut on purpose to provide a disturbing eight-legged embellishment for your party.

- Black paper
- Pencil
- Scissors

1. Fold the paper on the short side in an accordion style—the number of folds determines how many spiders will appear.

2. Draw a simple spider with thick legs on the front of the paper. Make sure four of the legs extend beyond the folded edges of the paper on both sides.

3. Carefully cut around the spider, making sure not to cut the folds where the legs go beyond the edges.

4. Open up the folded paper to reveal a paper chain of spiders.

5. Repeat for as many as you want, and use to decorate windows, walls, doors, or a Christmas tree.

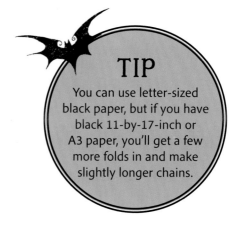

TIP
You can use letter-sized black paper, but if you have black 11-by-17-inch or A3 paper, you'll get a few more folds in and make slightly longer chains.

Scary Snowman

Snow in all its forms delights Jack when he tumbles into Christmas Town, including a snowman with coals for eyes and a candy-cane-handled umbrella that provides camouflage from elves that sleigh and slide through the streets. Jack saw only one snowman, but you can make as many as you want. Use as decor around the house, on a table, or even on your front steps.

- Craft knife or serrated knife
- Three Styrofoam balls in different sizes—small, medium, and large
- Wood skewers
- Glue (not hot glue)
- Black paint or black permanent markers
- Paintbrushes
- Ribbon
- Scissors
- Twigs in the shape of arms with fingers

1. Using the craft knife, slice a small amount off the bottom of the largest Styrofoam ball so it sits flat. Slice off an even smaller layer off the top. Do the same for the medium-sized ball. Flatten the bottom of the smallest ball, but do not flatten its top.

2. Using the wood skewers and glue, attach the three balls.

3. Once the snowman is assembled, use black paint to paint on fearsome eyes and a scary mouth. Jack's face would work well as an inspiration. Paint on coat buttons if you like.

4. Cut a piece of ribbon to wind around the neck as a scarf, and secure with glue.

5. Stick the twigs into the side of the middle ball on either side to make arms.

The Nightmare Before Christmas Ornaments

Halloween Town crafts its Christmas in a horror-made way, and so can your guests, by adding both cheer and fear to their own Christmas tree ornament.

- Empty ball ornaments (at least one per guest)
- Blank ceramic ornaments (at least one per guest)
- Plastic insects, spiders, bats, rats, snakes, mini pumpkins, cobwebs, etc.
- Stickers and glitter
- Permanent markers
- Paint and paintbrushes
- Christmas decorations such as ribbons, plastic holly berries, ivy leaves, bells, mini Santa hats
- String (optional)
- Hot glue

1. Set up a station for your partygoers to personalize ornaments. (You can use the same station for the Sandy Claws Hats and Soul-Taking Stockings.)
2. Empty ball ornaments can be filled with bugs, glitter, or spiderwebs. Blank ceramic ornaments can be drawn or painted on, and have stickers or glitter added.
3. Don't forget to add a bit of holiday cheer with the Christmas decorations.
4. Attach string with hot glue to bigger plastic snakes, pumpkins, or bats to be another type of ornament.
5. Decorate your party tree, or send them home with your guests as a favor.

Sandy Claws Hats and Soul-Taking Stockings

When Jack tries to explain the concept of holiday stockings, the citizens of Halloween Town don't understand why there wouldn't be a foot inside. More than likely they'd ask where Santa's head was if Jack had shown them his red hat! Guests can hang their stocking by the chimney (with care, if you have a fireplace) before they take them home. The hats can be worn as festive holiday attire during the party—after all, Jack realized the hat was all he needed to complete his Sandy Claws suit.

- Santa hats and holiday stockings (at least one per guest)
- Paint and paintbrushes
- Permanent markers
- Stickers and glitter
- Plastic insects, spiders, bats, rats, snakes, cobwebs, or other small scary elements
- Hot glue

1. Set up a station for your partygoers to personalize a hat or stocking (or both). Set out a few sample hats and stockings to inspire your guests.

Dreadful Snow Globes

Jack contemplates a large snow globe as the Halloween Town meeting ends, worrying that though everyone's excited, they don't seem to understand the Christmas holiday. They might have understood better if the globe contained something dreadful, not delightful. If you're distributing these as party favors, make them at least a day ahead of the occasion. If the guests are making these as a craft activity, be sure to remind them to allow the final product to dry for 24 hours before shaking or displaying.

- Small *Nightmare Before Christmas* toy or ornament (at least one per guest)
- Scissors
- Empty clean jars with lids (at least one per guest)
- Waterproof craft glue or epoxy
- Water
- Glitter
- Glycerin
- Teaspoon(s)
- Towel(s)

TIP

You can use any jars you'd like, but 4-ounce jars to 10-ounce jars work the best. Source rounded jars for that true snow globe look. Long or tall toys also work best.

1. If using an ornament, clip off the string first. Glue the toy or ornament to the inside of the jar lid, and allow to dry. If your ornament is a little short, you can glue a small piece of wood or plastic to the base of your toy to give it some additional height before gluing it to the lid.

2. Fill the jar with water, almost all the way to the top. Add 2 teaspoons glitter and 1 teaspoon glycerin. Add more water until the liquid is completely flush with the top of the jar.

3. Add a line of glue all the way around the inside of the lid. Screw the lid onto the jar—water will spill out as it overflows, so have a towel ready! Allow to dry for 24 hours. Shake and enjoy!

4. Make a glow-in-the-dark snow globe! Let some tonic water (with quinine) go completely flat by leaving it open for a few days. Use the flat tonic water instead of tap water in the snow globe, and shine a black light on the craft to see it glow.

Christmas/Halloween Photo Mash-Up

Jack gives Sally the coveted assignment of sewing the red suit with white trim he'll wear for Christmas. Jack shows her a portrait of himself in his pin-striped Pumpkin King suit, then places a translucent paper over it with a picture of Sandy's outfit so she can follow the pattern. With these two themed images over their own real-world photo, your guests can create their own vision for the holiday.

Include a note in your invitation that guests should bring a 4-by-6-inch photo of themselves, or have them email you a photo that you can then print out and have ready for the party. If you have a photo printer available to you, you can also take photos of guests as they arrive so no one is left out!

- Scissors
- Card stock or cardboard
- 4-by-6-inch photo of each guest
- Glue or rubber cement
- Vellum
- Hole punch
- Metal brads
- Markers or permanent markers
- Paper or cardboard frames to fit a 5-by-7-inch photo (optional)

1. Cut a piece of cardboard or card stock 5 inches by 7 inches so there is a half-inch border around a photo, then glue the photo in place.

2. Cut two 5 by 7 inch pieces of vellum and layer on top of the photo. Punch a hole through all three layers at the top center of the stack. Use a metal brad to hold it in place.

3. Turn one of the vellum sheets so it is out of the way. Use markers to draw a Halloween scene on the remaining vellum sheet.

4. Swap the pieces of vellum, only this time use the markers to draw a Christmas scene.

5. Flip or slide away the vellum to give the photo a Christmas or Halloween look, just like Jack.

6. Add a paper frame if you'd like to display your handiwork!

House of Christmas Cards

Upon his return from Christmas Town, Jack locks himself up in his tower, obsessed with trying to understand the secret of the holiday. He's surrounded himself with holiday trappings—toys and greenery and a house he built from Christmas cards. As he voices his fear that he doesn't understand the holiday as he should, the house of Christmas cards collapses. See if you can keep Jack's hopes from plummeting by competing to see who can build the tallest tower of holiday greetings.

- **Large number of Christmas cards that fold**

1. Gather up a large assortment of folding-style Christmas cards. They can be any size or design, and it's even better if they don't match.
2. Have the guests divide up into teams, and give each team an equal number of cards.
3. On the floor, have each team begin a house or tower made out of Christmas cards. The tallest house of cards that doesn't fall over wins!

White Elephant Gift-Giving Game

A white elephant gift is the worst kind you can get. The term "white elephant" refers to an impractical present the receiver cannot easily regift. On the party invitation, ask each guest to bring a wrapped box containing something pretty terrible. The giver should remain anonymous, and it's best to suggest a price limit. The gifts should be funny, weird, creepy, or completely ridiculous—this is not about receiving a sentimental or valuable present! It's about laughter and entertainment. It's also a competition to see who can give the worst possible gift!

- **One really terrible gift from each guest (wrapped but without the giver's name on it)**
- **Pen**
- **Small slips of paper**

As your party starts, gather the gifts and set them in one area, perhaps under a Christmas tree—but make sure they're separate from any other presents!

1. Write a number on each slip of paper, then have each guest draw until everyone is assigned a number. This is the order in which the gifts will be opened.

2. The guest who draws number 1 selects a gift and opens it. Make sure everyone can see each horrible thing inside the presents.

3. Each following giftee can either pick an unwrapped gift and open it, or swap it (unwrapped) for a gift that is already open.

4. A present can only be swapped once per turn, and an individual present can only be swapped three times total.

5. After all the guests have had a turn, the first guest can keep what they have or exchange it for someone else's gift, ending the game.

6. Once all the presents are opened and the game is over, the party host should act as judge and will determine which present is the creepiest. The guest who brought that gift is declared the winner.

Halloween Town Christmas Carols

Jack's intention to do Christmas the Halloween way includes the traditional carols played during the festivities. He even teaches the Halloween Town jazz band to play "Jingle Bells." Here's your chance to sing carols as Jack would want them—with plenty of gloom and doom.

- Pens and sheets of paper (at least one per guest)
- Prize

1. Give each guest a pen and paper. Ask them to think of a traditional Christmas carol (you might want to write up a list for them to review), then rewrite it as it would be sung in Halloween Town. For example, "Rudolph the Red-Nosed Reindeer" as "Zero the Orange-Nosed Ghost Dog." Or the night wouldn't be "Silent," it would be "Shrieking."

2. Have each guest write down their song variation and then perform it.

3. If you'd like to make it a competition, everyone can vote on who has the best Halloween Town song adaptation.

The Nightmare Before Christmas Creature Creator

From Lock, Shock, and Barrel to Oogie Boogie to Harlequin Demon, the inhabitants of Halloween Town have dark but clever names. What would your name be if you became a citizen? Here's an amusing way to find out!

- Creature Creator Name Generator template ⬇
- Printer
- Paper
- Poster board
- Markers
- Name tag stickers
- Safety pins (optional)

1. Download the Creature Creator Name Generator template from our Online Resources page ⬇, and print it out, or write the list on a piece of poster board or paper.

2. Have guests determine their creature moniker by using the name generator: The guest should use the first letter of their first name to determine their first creature descriptor, the first letter of the last name to determine their second descriptor, and their birth month to determine what type of creature they are.

3. Set out stickers and markers for guests to make name tags with their creature names to wear during the party.

4. Set out markers and paper for guests to draw creature self-portraits. Use the artwork to decorate the walls or pin them to guest's shirts.

Menu

SNACKS

- Jack Skellington Black Bean Dip (page 20)
- Oogie Boogie Guacamole With Ghost & Christmas Tree Chips (page 23)

STARTERS

- Snake and Spider Stew (page 32)

ENTRÉES

- Christmas Tree Empanadas (page 56)
- Man-Eating Wreath Burritos (page 58)

SIDES

- Roasted Jack-O'-Lantern Salad With Bloody Orange Vinaigrette (page 35)

DESSERTS

Birthday Party

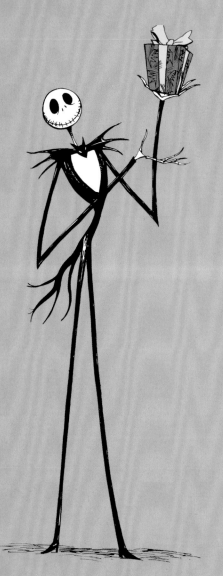

INVITATION

Jack Skellington Invitation

DECOR

Black Snowflakes and Gold Stars

Coffin Doors

Unhappy Gravestones and Jack-O'-Lanterns

Creepy Streamers and Gross
Confetti-Filled Balloons

CRAFTS AND FAVORS

Gummy-Worm-Filled Oogie Boogie

Make a Real-World Toy Scary

Haunted Gingerbread House

Paint on Sally's Stitches and Jack's Smile

ACTIVITIES

Never-Ending Wrapped Present

Skeleton Fingers Snowball Pickup

Pin the Birthday Hat on Jack Skellington

Oogie Boogie Piñata

MENU

Birthday Party

Birthdays occur throughout the year and should be celebrated whenever they fall, but no matter the season, there is no spookier birthday party than a *Nightmare Before Christmas* birthday party. It's three celebrations in one! Imagine what Jack Skellington would have done had he discovered a Birthday Town: substituting snakes for streamers and bugs for candy.

This fete is intended to help a child celebrate their special day, but adults are welcome to modify these ideas or pull in moments from other parties to create their own festive affair.

For the invitation, Jack dons a birthday hat decorated with colorful stickers, stripes, or polka dots while the decorations include party streamers in spooky color combos and smiling jack-o'-lanterns placed among tombstones reminiscent of the Halloween Town cemetery. Decorating your doors to look like coffins will put the fun in funereal, as will balloons filled with confetti fashioned into the shapes of spiders and bats. Black snowflakes give a nod to a Halloween Town–style Christmas, complemented by glittering gold stars.

Just as Jack instructs the townspeople to make Christmas their way, toys that would normally gleam are given a ghostly spin as guests are invited to paint a pull-toy with a monster's face or craft a teddy bear with stuffing seeping out.

Though the birthday celebrant receives the gifts, partygoers are not left empty-handed, as take-home party favors, crafts, and prizes abound. Everyone's favorite bogeyman is well represented, including a handmade, gummy-worm-filled Oogie Boogie. Don't forget to take photos of your guests with toothy Jack Skellington grins and Sally's stitched smiles and email them afterward for a picture-perfect memento.

Some Jack-approved birthday party games include pinning a hat on Jack Skellington and taking turns smashing an Oogie Boogie piñata filled with even more gummy candies. There is one present that everyone will get to unwrap, and unwrap, and unwrap, as it's covered in layers of alternating birthday, Halloween, and Christmas party paper.

Whether the celebration is for someone as young as Lock, Shock, or Barrel, or as old as Dr. Finkelstein, everyone will have a frightfully good time at this Halloween Town–style birthday bash.

Jack Skellington Invitation

Jack himself invites your guests to the birthday celebration with a colorful request for their presence, featuring his winsome visage. Encourage your guests to wear black-and-white pin-striped suits, colorful patchwork dresses, or any attire that would fit in with the Halloween Town theme, especially if you plan to have a face-painting station (page 166).

- Birthday Party Invitation template ⬇
- White printer paper or different colored card stock
- Printer
- Pens in your chosen color
- Scissors
- Glue
- Construction paper in multiple colors
- Glitter, pom-poms, confetti (optional)

1. Download the template from our Online Resources page ⬇, and print out enough copies for the number of guests you're inviting.

2. Write in your party details with a pen (Jack would probably prefer black), or type them up, print out the number you need, cut them to fit, and glue them onto the invites.

3. Using different colors of construction paper, cut out triangle-shaped party hats at an appropriate size to fit Jack's head on the invitation. Glue one each to the top of Jack's head. Decorate the hats if you'd like: sprinkle with glitter, draw on stripes or polka dots, or glue on pom-poms. You can also drop a few pieces of confetti into the envelope before sealing it. Bonus points if you can use Halloween-themed confetti!

4. Deliver these spooktacular invitations to your guests.

You're Invited!
To Jack's House for a Spooky Birthday Party!

Friday October 31 3pm
35657 Pumpkin Lane
Halloweentown
Wear a costume!

Decor

Black Snowflakes and Gold Stars

Once Santa Claus fixes the Christmas Jack has bungled, he flies his sleigh over Halloween Town and makes it snow there for the first time. This handmade precipitation of black snowflakes and gold stars mashes up the colors of both Christmas and Halloween towns for a dreadfully wonderful party canopy.

- Black construction paper
- Gold construction paper or card stock
- Pencil
- Scissors
- Monofilament
- Painter's tape or masking tape

1. To make the snowflakes and spiderwebs, start by cutting a sheet of black construction paper into a square. Fold diagonally to create a triangle with a sharp crease, and continue to fold in half, making triangles until the triangle is fairly narrow or you can't fold it any further.

2. For the snowflakes, cut off small pieces around the arrow shape, including some of the edges and corners. Feel free to experiment with different curves and angles. For the spiderwebs, round the edge and then cut out a pattern that is similar to a one-sided bare Christmas tree. When finished, gently unfold and flatten.

3. To make the stars, draw star shapes in varying shapes and sizes on a sheet of paper and cut out. Repeat until there are a coffin's-worth of snowflakes, spiderwebs, and stars.

4. Using the monofilament, hang these from the ceiling, or use tape to decorate your windows and walls.

Coffin Doors

Refashioning your doors to look like coffins is an easy way to bring a bit of Jack's coffin sleigh style to your party. This is particularly fun to do on closet doors: Put a skeleton inside for guests to see when they go to hang up their coats!

- Several sheets of black poster board (about 3 sheets per door)
- Pencil
- Scissors
- Painter's tape or masking tape

1. Choose the doors to be made into coffins—they should be easily visible from the main party space. Place a piece of poster board against the top inside corner of the doorway. Mark a diagonal line to create a triangle. Cut out the triangle, and then use this piece of posterboard to trace out a second, matching triangle.

2. Use another piece of black posterboard to create another, taller, thinner triangle to create the shape of the coffin. Once again, use this piece of poster board to trace and create a second matching triangle for the opposite side of the door. Depending on the shape of the door, a wide black strip of poster board may need to be added across the top to complete the coffin shape.

3. Tape each triangle—and the black strip of p oster board, if using—in place on the door. The black corners outline the shape of the coffin in the middle.

4. Draw the letters RIP about 12 inches tall on another sheet of poster board and cut out. Tape to the center of the coffin on the door.

Unhappy Gravestones and Jack-O'-Lanterns

Once Jack's work is completed for Halloween, he slips away to stroll among the angular gravestones of the town's cemetery in a melancholy manner, even though he feels this has been the most horrible holiday yet. Your guests can party in peace with these personalized tombstones and grimacing jack-o'-lanterns scattered around your party scape.

- Several sheets of foam core poster board in white, black, or gray
- Pencil
- Precision knife or scissors
- Permanent markers

- Several large pumpkins, real or fake
- Paint and paintbrushes (optional)
- Birthday hats

1. On a foam core poster board, draw the shape of a gravestone with the pencil, and carefully cut out the shape with a precision knife or scissors. Repeat with several different shapes and sizes, and mix up the colors if desired.

2. On the front of each gravestone, write things like "unhappy birthday," "grim greetings," "had too much fun," "ate too much cake," "happy boo-day," "dark lagoon leeches got him," or think of your own unhappy birthday greeting. You can also write your name and birthday on a gravestone, or the names and birthdays of your friends!

3. For the jack-o'-lantern heads, paint a face on each pumpkin with the permanent markers or paints. Make some happy, some sad, and some scary. Top with a birthday party hat.

4. Place the gravestones and jack-o'-lanterns around the party space, on the front porch, or in the yard leading up to the party.

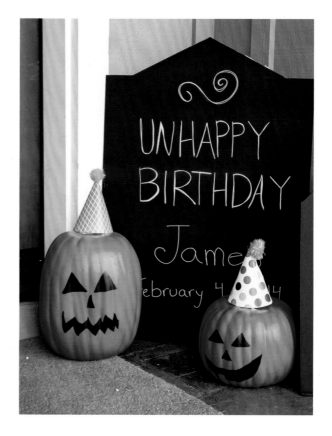

Creepy Streamers and Gross Confetti-Filled Balloons

Give your guests the heebie-jeebies with decorative streamers in creepy colors and balloons filled with gross-out glitter and shiver-inducing insects. LED lights or small glow sticks can offer a radiance akin to a full moon that will light up your celebration.

- Black, gray, gold, green, orange, purple, or brown streamers
- Tape
- Black, gray, white, green, orange, purple, and brown balloons
- Clear balloons
- String, ribbons, or black twine
- Funnel or tube
- Spider or Halloween confetti, glitter, and/or small plastic bugs or eyeballs
- Small glow sticks or LED lights (optional)

1. Hang the streamers from the ceiling, doorways, or across your windows. The streamers can hang straight down from the ceiling, or you can mix in them in and around other decorations. They can also be twisted across doorways, windows, or walls. Combine multiple colors of streamers together in a twist to make it colorful, or keep with the unhappy birthday theme and use only black, white, brown, and gray.

2. Mix in color balloons as desired. Fill the balloons with helium and tie to chairs, or fill with air and scatter around the floor. Balloons can also be tied to the ends of streamers hanging from the ceiling.

3. For the clear balloons, put the end of a funnel or tube into the uninflated balloon. Pour confetti, glitter, or small plastic bugs into the balloon. For an evening or nighttime party, you can add small glowsticks or LED lights. Remove the funnel, inflate balloon with air or helium, and tie it off. Place these all around the party space.

Gummy-Worm-Filled Oogie Boogie

During the battle to save Sally and Sandy Claws from Oogie Boogie, Jack grabs a loose thread on the burlap sack that encompasses the ghastly ghoul, and it unravels, spilling out worms and bugs and all manner of creepy-crawlies. No jokin' here, partygoers will love the sweets inside this sinister Boogie man.

- Burlap
- Scissors
- Black permanent marker
- Gummy worms (at least a handful per guest)
- Individual plastic bags (at least one per guest)
- String (optional)
- Needle and black thread, or hot glue

1. Fold a piece of burlap in half, and draw the shape of Oogie Boogie on the front, 6 to 12 inches high. Using sharp scissors, carefully cut out the shape (keeping the fabric folded) to get two matching pieces.

2. Using the black permanent marker, draw Oogie's empty triangular eyes and gaping mouth on the front piece.

3. Fill an individual plastic bag with a handful of gummy worms. If your bags are zip-top bags, simply zip them shut. If not, tie them shut with a bit of string.

4. Insert the bag of gummy worms between the two pieces of burlap, then stitch or hot-glue the two pieces together, leaving the head unsealed. If you are stitching, loosely stitch Oogie's head together with a new piece of thread. If you are using hot glue, simply leave his head unglued.

5. Make one for each guest to take home as a favor. Guests can pull on the thread to open, or better yet, rip Oogie Boogie apart to reveal the treats inside!

Make a Real-World Toy Scary

When Jack decides to make Christmas his way, the citizens of Halloween Town are enlisted to create toys that will make the children in the real world scream like a banshee in terror! The amount of scare you or your guests can bring to these toys is limited only by your nightmares. You can make these in advance as decoration, or you can set up a crafting station for guests to make their own during the party and take home as a spooky favor.

- Selection of toys including rubber ducks, jack-in-the-boxes, nutcrackers, or teddy bears
- Permanent markers
- Paint and paintbrushes
- Needle and thread

- Scissors
- Plastic bugs and creatures
- Toy skeleton bones, hands, skulls, and spiderwebs
- Hot glue

1. Revamp(ire) the toys, particularly the rubber ducks and nutcrackers, by drawing on nasty, menacing eyes or sharp-looking fangs with the markers or paint.

2. For the teddy bears, carefully cut off the head, arms, or legs of the bear, or cut up the middle. Pull out a bit of the stuffing, and reassemble whatever you've cut by stitching it back together— badly!— with needle and thread.

3. For the jack-in-the-box, open the box and replace or modify the toy inside the box. You can replace the toy inside completely with a skull or skeleton hand for a frightful surprise. Decorate the outside of the box with dark colors or chilling images.

4. For any or all of the toys, feel free to hot-glue plastic bugs, snakes, or rats on them for extra menace.

5. Don't take these steps as your only options—feel free to get as creative as Jack.

Haunted Gingerbread House

Decorating a gingerbread house is a delicious tradition of the Christmas holiday, but if you're doing a birthday celebration Jack's way, a haunted gingerbread house is the perfect way to honor both holidays at your party. Decorate one to use as decor, or pre-assemble several houses and set up a decorating station with sinister-looking candy for your guests to complete.

- Gingerbread house kit, including cookie house pieces and icing, plus extra icing for decorating
- Candy for decoration: gummy worms, eyeballs, gummy bats, bones, candy corn, candy pumpkins, sprinkles, black licorice, chocolate bars, gumdrops, wax teeth, candy bugs, etc.
- Muffin pan
- Chocolate sandwich cookies (optional)
- Large plastic zipper bag (optional)
- Bowl(s) (optional)

1. Assemble the gingerbread house(s) as directed on a solid base.
2. If your guests will be doing the decorating, put a selection of candies in the muffin cups for them to use.
3. If you'd like a front yard or backyard (or graveyard) around your house, put chocolate sandwich cookies in the plastic zipper bag, and smash until fine, to make cookie dirt. Put this in a bowl for your guests to use if they're running their own construction crew.
4. Using any extra icing (or make extra since you know you'll probably take a taste or three), secure a layer of cookie dirt to the base. Decorate the house and the base with the additional icing and candies to make a spooky yet sweet haunted house.

Paint on Sally's Stitches and Jack's Smile

Among the most iconic images in *The Nightmare Before Christmas* are Jack's endlessly deep eyes and beguiling grin and Sally's stitched-on smile and eyelashes. Your guests can become a gathering of Jacks and Sallys by giving them a peculiar makeover. Encourage your guests to wear black-and-white pin-striped suits or ragdoll-like colorful dresses to complement these Jack and Sally looks by including a request for themed attire on the party invitation.

- Large makeup brushes or makeup sponges, plus fine-tipped detail brushes
- Face or body paint in white, light blue, dark blue, gray, black, and red
- Eye shadow in black, dark blue, and white (optional)
- Black liquid eyeliner (optional)

1. Paint each attendee's face with a white base layer for Jack or a light blue base layer for Sally to make sure the paint really stands out. Dab on the paint with a large makeup brush or a makeup sponge to avoid streaks.
2. To add depth, use eye shadow or dab paint (gray for Jack and dark blue for Sally) around the hairline, jawline, sides of the nose, and cheekbones.
3. Use white paint or white eye shadow to highlight the bridge of the partygoer's nose.
4. Paint on big black eyes for Jack or long eyelashes and red lips for Sally.
5. For Jack's smile and Sally's stitches, use a fine paintbrush and black paint, or use black liquid eyeliner for even more control. For an additional 3D effect, use white paint and a fine-tipped brush to layer white on top of the black stitches.
6. Take photos!

Never-Ending Wrapped Present

Upon his return from Christmas Town, Jack calls a town meeting to explain his new discoveries, one of which is a present. As he explains it, it starts with a box, which is then covered in shiny wrapping paper. Nothing delights children and adults more than opening a wrapped present—unless it takes forever to get down to the gift!

- Tape
- Gift or prize in a box
- Halloween wrapping paper
- Christmas wrapping paper
- Birthday wrapping paper
- Scissors
- Ribbon or bow (optional)

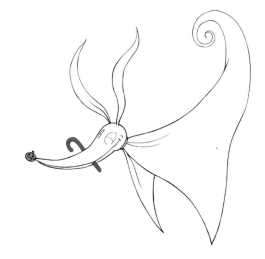

1. Tape your gift box shut, and wrap the box as you would any present, but with many, many alternating layers of Halloween, Christmas, and birthday wrapping paper. The more layers of paper, the longer the game will last. Finish decorating the box with ribbons or a bow.

2. With your guests sitting in a circle, and starting with the birthday celebrant, have each person remove a layer of wrapping paper and then pass to the person next to them, going around and around. Whoever removes the last layer of paper and opens the box wins the gift inside!

Skeleton Fingers Snowball Pickup

When Jack tumbles into Christmas Town, he's enthralled by the trappings of the season—including, as he sings, "children throwing snowballs instead of throwing heads!" With his bony fingers, does Jack even have a chance to pick up a snowball, much less throw it? Here's your guests' chance to try

- Large jar
- Cotton balls
- Timer
- Masking tape
- Chopsticks, at least two pairs, split

1. On a table, set out the jar, and spread the cotton balls (snowballs) all around. Have a timer ready.

2. Use the masking tape to tape one chopstick toward the end of each finger on the player, giving them four "skeleton" fingers.

3. Hit the timer for one minute, and yell "go!" (Or "boo!") Have the player pick up as many of the cotton balls as possible with their skeleton fingers and place them in the jar. The player who gets the most snowballs in the jar within one minute wins the game and gets a prize.

4. To keep the game moving, get additional sets of chopsticks and have one guest putting on their fingers while another is playing the game.

Pin the Birthday Hat on Jack Skellington

If there had been a door for a Birthday Town for Jack to pass through in *The Nightmare Before Christmas*, he would have surely fallen in love with this iconic contest, played by children of all ages. Why has this party game—where you're blindfolded and disoriented before playing—been popular for so long? Because it's scary! And lots of fun.

- Pin the Hat on Jack template ⬇
- White printer paper
- Printer
- Scissors
- Glue
- Large white poster board
- Tape
- Construction paper in multiple colors
- Markers
- Pom-poms or glitter (optional)
- Glue dots
- Blindfold

1. Locate the template on our Online Resources page ⬇, and print it as large as possible. Cut out and glue to the poster board and tape to a wall, low enough for the players to reach the target. You can also draw the image of Jack directly on the poster board.

2. Using the different colors of construction paper, cut out several triangle-shaped party hats at an appropriate size to fit Jack's head. If desired, decorate the hats with polka dots, stripes, glitter, or pom-poms to make each one distinct.

3. Label each hat with the player's name using the markers, and attach a glue dot to the back.

4. One at a time, blindfold a player and hand them their hat. Turn the player around a few times, then point them in the right direction. The player who sticks their hat closest to the top of Jack's head wins a prize!

Oogie Boogie Piñata

Oogie Boogie loves games. When he captures Sandy Claws, and then Sally, he traps them in his lair—a creepy gambling den filled with torturous devices that can turn his prisoners into a soup or stew. So here's a chance to get some revenge on the boogiest of bogeymen.

- Black permanent marker
- Two large pieces of cardboard
- Scissors or precision knife
- Paintbrush and glow-in-the-dark paint (optional)
- Hole punch
- Twine
- Individual bags of gummy worms, gummy spiders, or gummy bugs
- Rope
- Black light (optional)
- Blindfold
- Plastic baseball bat

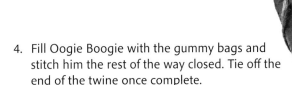

1. Using a permanent marker, draw the shape of Oogie Boogie on one piece of cardboard and cut out. Using the first piece as a template, trace around the shape on the other piece of cardboard, and cut out.

2. Give Oogie Boogie a face by drawing it on with the marker. You can do this in glow-in-the-dark paint to make him even more eerie.

3. Using the hole punch, punch parallel holes all the way around both pieces, including one at the top of his head. Stitch together with the twine, but leave a couple of inches around his head open so you can insert the bags of gummy worms. Don't cut the twine just yet.

4. Fill Oogie Boogie with the gummy bags and stitch him the rest of the way closed. Tie off the end of the twine once complete.

5. Punch a larger hole at the top of Oogie's head and attach the rope to the top of his head and hang from a tree outside. If the party is at night, aim a black light at him so he can glow in the dark. For added glow-in-the-dark fun, paint the blindfold and plastic baseball bat with glow-in-the-dark paint as well.

6. Taking turns, blindfold each player and have them take a few swings at Oogie Boogie with the baseball bat. When Oogie Boogie is defeated, all his worms will spill out!

Menu

SNACKS

- The Mayor Chocolate Pretzel Spiderwebs (page 17)
- Full Moon Queso Dip (page 24)

STARTERS

- Worm's Wort and Frog's Breath Soup (page 33)

ENTRÉES

- Mummy Boy Dogs (page 46)
- Christmas Tree Veggie Pizza With Spiders (page 49)

SIDES

- Harlequin Demon Sweet Potato Fries With Ranch Dressing (page 36)

DESSERTS

- Man-Eating Marshmallow Crispy Wreaths (page 64)
- Christmas Town Gingerbread Snowflakes With Spiders (page 68)
- Sally Patchwork Layer Cake (page 96)

DRINKS

- Halloween Town Band Zombie Mocktail (page 106)
- Frog's Breath Floats (page 106)

Zero the Dog
Summer BBQ Party

INVITATION
Ghost Dog Bone Invitation

DECOR
Ghostly Balloons
Zero's Tombstone Doghouse
Holiday Trees Portal Doors
Glue-Soaked Ghost Dogs

CRAFTS AND FAVORS
Dearly Departed Dog Costume
Zero Ears and Glowing Pumpkin Nose
Black Cat Dog Toy

ACTIVITIES
Bones in the Graveyard Scavenger Hunt
Bobbing for Jack-O'-Lanterns
Cornhole With Dog Toys
Holiday Tug-of-War

MENU

Zero the Dog Summer BBQ Party

There's nothing like having a party outdoors in the summertime, and it's even better when you're surrounded by your canine friends. Zero's Summer BBQ Party celebrates the connection we have with our dogs—ever playful and always faithful. Even though shadows and spirits permeate Halloween Town, nothing stops Zero, Jack Skellington's devoted little ghost dog, in his utter joy when he's by Jack's side. In fact, Zero comes to Jack's rescue before Christmas even starts. Without Zero's glowing pumpkin nose to light his way, Jack would not have been able to drive his sleigh.

This party is designed to celebrate Jack's canine companion with a pet-friendly gathering. However, dogs are not required, and there are plenty of delightful things for humans to do as well.

For the invitation, Zero sends out a bone-shaped request. You could even make two—one for your human guests and one for their dogs.

Jack discovers "someplace new" when he takes a melancholy walk after Halloween and finds himself in a circular grove of trees. Each tree trunk bears a door shaped to represent the holiday town within. Jack's intrigued by the depictions—and then sees the colorful door to Christmas Town, whereupon his smile grows from ear to ear (if he had ears, of course). By painting the icons of each holiday onto the trees in your party space, your guests will enjoy the same joyous feeling as Jack as he ponders the possibilities of what each door represents.

Zero would feel as if he's in his own boneyard when you set a cardboard version of his tombstone doghouse in your party scape. You'll craft balloons designed to float like ghosts throughout the party and you can create a few ghostly canines out of just cheesecloth and glue. You can use these as decor, craft some during the party, or hand out the ones you've made as favors. Pre-party planning reminder: The glue-soaked ghost dogs will need a day or two to dry.

A Halloween Town twist has the dogs bobbing for jack-o'-lanterns (tennis balls) and humans bobbing for apples among other fun activities. The crafts, games, and savory barbecued fare served at Zero's Summer Barbecue Party will provide all participants with a tail-wagging good time.

Ghost Dog Bone Invitation

It's Zero's turn to invite party guests, in the form of a bone any ghost dog would love to gnaw. Be sure to include anything your guests need to know in order to make final arrangements for your party!

- Ghost Dog Bone Invitation template ⬇
- Ivory or white card stock
- Printer
- Hole punch
- Scissors
- White cheesecloth
- Large envelopes (optional)

1. Download the template from our Online Resources page ⬇. You can size it to fit one per sheet or two per sheet. Add party details (or handwrite later), and print as many as needed on the card stock.

2. Use the hole punch to punch two holes at the top of each page above the center of the bone.

3. Cut several small strips of cheesecloth. Thread one through the holes on each invitation. Tie a bow in the front.

4. Place in a large envelope or hand-deliver to your doggie guests.

Zero Invites You To Follow Him to a BBQ!
Location: The Holiday Woods
Time: 1pm to 4pm

Ghostly Balloons

Zero floats along like a bobbing balloon as he follows Jack Skellington around Halloween Town. These balloons are more human than dog, but like the ghosts that greet visitors to Zero's favorite holiday, they'll make the scene so that it screams "This is Halloween."

- Helium tank
- White balloons
- Monofilament
- Black permanent marker
- White streamers
- Cheesecloth
- Scissors
- Black felt
- Glue or double-stick tape

1. Inflate some balloons with helium and other balloons with air. You can buy a helium tank or get balloons filled at your local party supply store. Tie off the balloons, and use the monofilament as string.

2. For the helium balloons, draw on eyes and a mouth with the black marker. Attach white streamers to the bottom of the balloons in various lengths. Tie the balloons to tables, chairs, or other places around the party space with the monofilament.

3. For the air-filled balloons, turn one upside down, holding it by the tie-off knot. Drape cheesecloth over the balloon, with more hanging down to create a good ghostly figure. Cut off any excess. Make a small hole in the center of the cheesecloth (careful—don't pop the balloon!) to allow for the knot of the balloon to come through, and tie on the monofilament as string. Cut out felt circles to use as the eyes and mouth, and carefully attach with glue or double stick tape to the cheesecloth. Hang the ghosts from the trees around the party scene.

4. If you have extra pieces of gauze, hang them from the trees or along fences as well to float in the breeze and add to the spooky atmosphere.

Zero's Tombstone Doghouse

Zero often rests in peace in a doghouse in the Halloween Town cemetery. As Jack walks through the graves at Halloween's end, he motions for Zero and the little ghost dog floats up to frolic at his side. This tombstone pays tribute to a skeleton's best friend.

- Large cardboard box, one side taped shut
- Scissors
- Large piece of cardboard
- Black permanent marker
- Black and/or gray paint or spray paint
- White paint (optional)
- Paintbrush
- Fake spiderwebs
- Glue

1. Carefully cut the flaps off the box, and then turn it upside down. Cut out a large, arched doorway on the short side of the box.

2. Measure the width of the side of the box with the arch, then trace a triangle on the separate piece of cardboard so that its bottom edge is wider than box's width—depending on your box's specifications, the flaps you've removed from the long side of the box may be just the right size. Cut out the triangle, and glue above the arched opening.

3. Using the markers or paint, paint the house black or gray and write "Zero" above the open arch. You can also add a cardboard cross at the top of the triangle, or paint roof tiles on the triangular part.

4. If you'd like, you can paint the entire piece of cardboard one color with paint or spray paint, then use white paint to add Zero's name or any other details to the doghouse.

5. Add spiderwebs or other decorations for a real graveyard feel.

6. Make multiple dog houses for decor, or for additional doggie guests.

Holiday Trees Portal Doors

Under a smiling jack-o'-lantern sunrise, Jack Skellington comes upon a circle of trees, each sporting a holiday icon. "What is this?" he asks himself. Each tree opens onto a world dedicated to celebrating a specific holiday. It's easy to create your own Hinterland of holiday doors—and a great place for memorable photos.

This decor concept works best with natural trees growing near your party site, but if that isn't available to you, get creative! If you're in a backyard, consider decorating a wooden fence or other nearby structures.

- Washable paints or chalk paints
- Paintbrushes
- Scissors
- Gold card stock
- Masking tape

1. Find six trees in a row or a circle near the party site.

2. Each tree gets painted with one of the holiday door icons. In order, they are: a large heart, a shamrock, an Easter egg, a jack-o'-lantern, a turkey, and a Christmas tree. If there aren't enough trees, just choose your favorite holidays! And if there are more than enough trees, add icons for your own favorites.

3. Make a doorknob for each tree by cutting out a circle 2 to 3 inches in diameter from the gold card stock. Stick each on the right side of the icon on a holiday tree.

4. Go further by adding decorations to each tree for its specific holiday. For instance, you can place Easter eggs beneath the Easter tree or a stuffed turkey at the foot of the Thanksgiving tree, or you can hang hearts from the Valentines tree or shamrocks from the branches of the St. Patrick's Day tree. Guests will be able to skip between holiday worlds by using the portals, and pose for a fun photo op.

Glue-Soaked Ghost Dogs

If Dr. Finkelstein created a dog, these glue-soaked ghost dogs would be the optimal companion for him. Being stiff as a corpse, they can't get free at all, unlike Sally. Here, you can make big dogs or tiny puppies—just make sure you have enough cheesecloth to cover their entire coat. These spectral hounds need to be constructed a day or two in advance in order to become dry as a bone.

- Plastic tablecloth or plastic liner
- Cardboard or card stock
- Masking tape
- Cheesecloth
- Scissors
- White glue
- Water
- Large bowl and mixing spoon
- Good length of craft wire
- Black permanent marker or black felt
- Colored ribbon
- Orange pom-pom
- String or monofilament (optional)

1. Cover a surface with a plastic tablecloth or plastic liner.

2. Crumple up cardboard or card stock to make the rough shape of a dog's body. Then scrunch up a little more cardboard to make a dog's head, including its nose. Use masking tape to hold each shape together. Don't worry about getting things perfect, the cardboard will eventually be removed from these two pieces.

3. Drape cheesecloth over the dog body form. Make sure it covers the entire form with some extra hanging down on the sides and back. Layer cheesecloth over the dog's head and nose. Cut off any extra cheesecloth, and if needed, cut a slit up the front to make sure your ghost dog has enough fabric for two front paws. Cut two smaller pieces of cheesecloth, with a point on the ends, to make ears.

4. In a large bowl, combine one part glue and one part water. Mix well.

5. Soak all the cheesecloth pieces that make up the ghost dog's body in the glue-water mixture—set aside the pieces for the ears so you don't lose them. Re-drape the dog body form with its precut cheesecloth—but don't worry if you don't put them exactly where you had them in the first place. Shape edges and a tail to achieve your dog's look. Drape the remaining cheesecloth over the dog's head and nose.

6. Cut two small pieces of wire, and stick them into the top of the dog body form (where the head should go!). Use the wires to attach the head to the body. Soak and then layer the strips for the ears on the dog. You can stick wires into the dog's head in the same way to support its ears if you don't want floppy ears.

7. Allow to dry undisturbed overnight.

8. Once completely dry, draw eyes on the face with black permanent marker, or glue on pieces of black felt. Wrap a small piece of ribbon around the neck, and secure it with a dab of glue as a collar. Attach the orange nose with a small amount of glue.

9. Gently remove the forms from underneath the cheesecloth. Remove the wires if you used them to support the ears. The dogs are so light that you can thread a piece of monofilament or string at various points through the dog to hang them so they float. Alternately, set on a table as decor.

10. Be sure to take them on plenty of long walks through cemeteries!

Dearly Departed Dog Costume

While black cats are typically loners, dogs are social creatures and like hanging around together. Here's a chance to provide Zero with companions by dressing up your own or the other tail-wagging partygoers as ethereal ghost dogs. Don't forget to reward your doggie friends with a treat for their patience!

- White fabric or sheet
- Marker
- Dog collar
- Scissors
- Hole punch (optional)
- Zip ties (optional)

1. Drape the white fabric over your dog to determine approximately how much will be needed. Mark where the fabric meets the ground in front of his or her paws, where it ends right after their tail, and where it falls on the front and back of the neck. Remove the material from the dog.

2. On the fabric, draw a rough oval from the front to the back. Use the dog collar as a template to draw a circle around where the head will poke through. Using the large oval you drew, trim the fabric to its final shape. Cut out the center circle for the head and neck.

3. Cut small holes around the neck opening, or use a hole punch so you can attach the costume to the collar.

4. Put the dog collar back on the dog. Slip the fabric over the dog's head and adjust so the shorter end is in front. Use the zip ties to attach the collar to the fabric through the holes.

5. Try not to be too scared of your new ghostly companion!

Zero Ears and Glowing Pumpkin Nose

Sally tries to stop Jack from piloting his "sleigh" by pouring Fog Juice into the town center's fountain. Consumed by a haze thicker than jelly brains, Jack worries that the reindeer can't see and therefore can't fly. But Zero comes to the rescue with his glowing orange nose to light Jack's way! Wearing your own shining snout will move you to the head of the team.

- Scissors
- White fabric or cheesecloth
- Hot glue or needle and thread
- White headbands (at least one per guest)
- Mini LED pumpkin lights
- Dress tape or double-sided medical adhesive

1. For the ears: Cut two long strips of fabric or cheesecloth about 12 inches long. Cut a point on each end.

2. Hot-glue or stitch each strip to the top of the headband.

3. For the nose: Apply a little dress tape to the bottom of the LED pumpkin, and stick to your nose. Add the headband ears, and match your best buddy for all eternity.

Black Cat Dog Toy

Black cats prowl the streets of Halloween Town, jumping on trash cans and slinking in the shadows. But your dogs won't find these feline figures alarming—they're charming, and any nearby cats will be glad nearby dogs have these playful toys.

- Black burlap (larger than 18 inches square)
- Scissors
- Pins (optional)
- Needle and black thread, or nontoxic hot glue
- One 17-ounce plastic water bottle, empty
- Batting
- White chalk or white fabric pen

1. Fold the piece of burlap in half and draw the shape of a black cat on the front, 12 to 18 inches high. Make the cat shape large enough to accommodate the height and width of the water bottle—be sure to add a couple of inches to the side of the cat so the cat will be able to fully wrap around the bottle. Cut out the shape with the fabric still folded to get two matching pieces. You might want to pin the top and bottom of the open side of the folded fabric, so it doesn't slip around.

2. Stitch or hot-glue together three sides of the cat, but be sure the fourth side is still wide enough for the water bottle to fit. Place a little batting at the bottom of the cat, then slide the empty water bottle between the two pieces of fabric. Fill in the rest of the space around the water bottle and above it with the batting. Once the cat is fully stuffed, seal it with stitches or glue.

3. Draw on a face, including cat eyes and whiskers, and any other details to fill out this feline.

4. Make one for each doggie guest to take home as a favor or to play with at the party. No real cats are harmed in the making of this toy!

Bones in the Graveyard Scavenger Hunt

As Zero follows Jack out of the cemetery, he barks his eagerness to play fetch with Jack. Jack is not in the mood, but Zero cannot be ignored, and so Jack throws him a bone—one of his ribs, actually. This scavenger hunt turns the tables on a familiar game—it's the humans who must fetch the bones for the dogs.

Alternatively, if you're only having humans at this party, create little goodie bags filled with candies and hide them around the party area.

- Bone-shaped dog biscuits
- Basket or pail, one for each guest

1. Prior to your guests' arrival, hide a lot of bone-shaped dog biscuits around the party space. (You might want to keep a count of how many, so you know they've all been found before the game ends.)

2. Gather guests together, and give each a basket or pail. On the count of three, have each guest—with or without help from their canine counterparts—find as many bones as they can until all are found.

3. The person or team who finds the most bones wins! Give them a delicious doggie treat or two to take home.

Bobbing for Jack-O'-Lanterns

Bobbing for apples was all the Halloween rage in years past, when the number of tries it took to snag some fruit from a basin of water signified how long it would take to snag a partner. Good thing they didn't use the pumpkins for that! This game does, in a way. The jack-o'-lanterns bobbed for here are made from tennis balls, so your dog won't need a mouth as large as the Clown with the Tear-Away Face to recover them.

If you only have humans at this party, or if humans want to play as well, get a second large bucket or beverage tub, place it on a chair, and let the humans bob for apples!

- Tennis balls
- Apples (optional, for adults)
- Black permanent marker
- Large bucket or beverage tub
- Water
- Timer

1. On each tennis ball, draw a different jack-o'-lantern face with the permanent marker.

2. Fill the bucket or tub with water, and add the tennis balls.

3. One at a time, have each dog guest take turns bobbing for jack-o'-lantern balls. After each turn, return the balls to the water. The dog that gets the most balls out of the water in three minutes wins the game.

4. If the humans are participating in a bob-for-apples competition, be sure to have plenty of fresh apples on hand.

Cornhole With Dog Toys

There are as many thoughts as to how the cornhole game came about as there are dog breeds. Historians are pretty sure the game went national in the early 2000s, out of Cincinnati, where it was known as the "tailgate toss" and played in parking lots at NFL games. "Tailgate" might be more applicable here, as part of the challenge is trying to get a dog toy through the round hole.

- Cornhole board(s)
- 8 cornhole bags (per board)
- 8 assorted dog toys
- Scoreboard or score keeper

1. Set up the cornhole boards 10 to 20 feet apart, depending on the level of difficulty you want. Divide guests into teams of two. Each team gets four bags and four dog toys.

2. Have each team alternate taking turns throwing a cornhole bag at the hole in the board, one player at a time. One bag on the board earns one point, one bag in the hole earns three points. Alternatively, you can play with slightly more official rules, and each team can take turns trying to knock the other's bags or toys off the board.

3. After each player's turn, have the player select one dog toy and throw. A dog toy on the board earns three points, and a dog toy in the hole earns five points.

4. A team loses a point if a dog guest steals a bag or a toy! The first team to reach 21 points wins.

Holiday Tug-of-War

Tug-of-war has been around *forever*, practiced all around the world, but it has been a sport only since the Olympic games in ancient Greece. *Dog* tug-of-war has probably also been around for as long, and both dogs and humans will get a chance to show off their skills in this holiday-themed game. Are you Team Halloween or Team Christmas?

- 10 to 20 feet of rope, or longer depending on number of guests
- Halloween ribbon
- Christmas ribbon
- Spray chalk

1. Tie a knot on each end of the rope and one in the center. On either side of the knot in the center of the rope, tie a piece of Christmas ribbon and a piece of Halloween ribbon.

2. Use the spray chalk to mark a line on the ground, about 4 feet long.

3. Form human guests into teams of two, or put together one-on-one dog teams. One side is Team Christmas, and the other side is Team Halloween.

4. Have each team, or each dog, pull on the rope until they pull the other team over the line. The stronger team or dog wins!

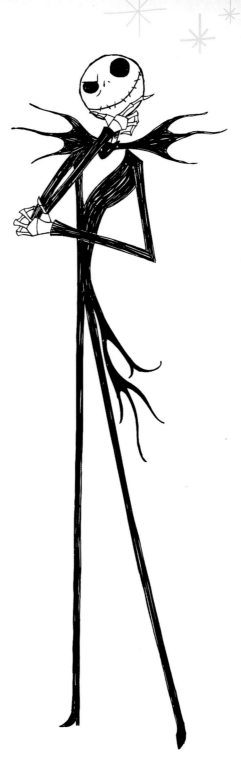

Menu

SNACKS

- Sally Sweet-n-Salty Popcorn (page 14)
- Igor Cheesy Breadstick Bones (page 18)

STARTERS

- Roasted Jack-O'-Lantern Salad With Bloody Orange Vinaigrette (page 35)

ENTRÉES

- Zero Barbecued Ribs (page 60)

SIDES

- Full Moon Mashed Potatoes (page 37)

DESSERTS

DRINKS

INSIGHT EDITIONS

PO Box 3088
San Rafael, CA 94912
www.insighteditions.com

Find us on Facebook: www.facebook.com/InsightEditions

Follow us on Twitter: @insighteditions

Library of Congress Cataloging-in-Publication Data available.

ISBN: 978-1-64722-534-6

Publisher: Raoul Goff
VP of Licensing and Partnerships: Vanessa Lopez
VP of Creative: Chrissy Kwasnik
VP of Manufacturing: Alix Nicholaeff
Editorial Director: Vicki Jaeger
Senior Designer: Judy Wiatrek Trum
Design Support: Monique Narboneta
Editor: Amanda Ng
Associate Editor: Anna Wostenberg
Production Editor: Jennifer Bentham
Senior Production Manager: Greg Steffen
Senior Production Manager, Subsidiary Rights: Lina s Palma

Photography by Tyler Chartier
Food Styling by Elena Craig
Prop Styling by Caroline Hall

Thank you to Kelsey for assisting on photography, Sreed for providing his beautiful
home for the photography location, and Megan and August for helping with cooking
and baking.

Thank you to our models Andrew, Amanda, Ashley, August, Beau, Erin, Julie, Monique,
Penn, Zoe, and Izzy the dog.

ROOTS of PEACE   REPLANTED PAPER

Insight Editions, in association with Roots of Peace, will plant two trees for each tree
used in the manufacturing of this book. Roots of Peace is an internationally renowned
humanitarian organization dedicated to eradicating land mines worldwide and
converting war-torn lands into productive farms and wildlife habitats. Roots of Peace will
plant two million fruit and nut trees in Afghanistan and provide farmers there with the
skills and support necessary for sustainable land use.

Manufactured in China by Insight Editions

10 9 8 7 6 5 4 3 2 1